AskMen.com Presents

FROM THE BAR
TO THE BEDROOM

AskMen.com Presents

FROM THE BAR
TO THE BEDROOM

THE 11 RULES FOR PICKING UP
AND PLEASURING WOMEN

EDITED BY JAMES BASSIL

Collins

An Imprint of HarperCollinsPublishers

Portions of this book have previously appeared on the AskMen.com Web site.

Contributors:
Luis Rodrigues
Jake Brennan
Armando Gomez
Justin Becker
Ryan Murphy
Andrea Gourgy
Roberto Rocha
Kyle Darbyson
Ian Harrison
Matthew Fitzgerald
Ben Dutka
Alex White
Rosy Saadeh
Jessica Lloyd
Drew Mayes
Anastasia Kolokotsas
Dr. Victoria Zdrok

Editorial consultation by MudScout.com
Interior illustrations: Sherwin Tjia.
Chapter header illustrations: © iStockphoto.com

FIRST EDITION

Designed by Jaime Putorti

Library of Congress Cataloging-in-Publication Data

AskMen.com from the bar to the bedroom : the 11 rules for picking up and pleasuring women / edited by James Bassil.--1st ed.
    p. cm.
  ISBN: 978-0-06-120852-2
  ISBN-10: 0-06-120852-3
  1. Sex instruction for men.   2. Dating (Social customs) I. Bassil, James. II. Ask Men.com.   III. Title: From the bar to the bedroom.
HQ36.A74 2007
646.7'7081—dc22

                  2006051923

07 08 09 10 11 WBT/BVG 10 9 8 7 6 5 4 3 2 1

CONTENTS

LIST OF ILLUSTRATIONS

INTRODUCTION

Since 1999, AskMen.com has been in the business of giving guys advice. We've counseled men on an ever-expanding series of topics, from how to dress, to how to behave in business meetings, to how to stock their fridges. As trends have come and gone, the areas in which our readers have sought guidance have shifted—during the "metrosexual" period of the early '00s, finding a good toner was a top-tier concern. Today, most men could care less.

Of course, some male concerns are ongoing staples. And on that list of ever-present inquiries, the issue of finding success with women has always hovered near the top. This isn't necessarily because men think about sex and dating more than they do their health, their social life, or their careers. It does, however, likely have a great deal to do with the fact that we guys don't like to reveal our own ignorance when it comes to picking up women. Quite the opposite: We'll boast to each other about our conquests, even as we secretly puzzle over how the hell we're going to land the next one.

Some men respond to this confusion by bemoaning its source: Why is it on me to approach and seduce her? Why can't she ever ask me out? Other men acknowledge that, fair or not, the expectation that we do the courting hasn't changed, and it's not about to any time soon. So rather than waiting on the sidelines for the gender roles to reverse, these are the guys that suck it up and start refining their skills. They do so by joining the millions that read the advice at AskMen.com, and they do so by reading books like this one.

You've chosen the right tool to refine your skills with. In this book, you will find eleven cardinal rules you need to follow to master the art of meeting, seducing, and pleasuring women. By the time you flip the last page, you'll be thoroughly versed in the art of approaching, talking to, and, ultimately, seducing women. And you won't disappoint once you get them back to your place, having absorbed the information on foreplay and sexual techniques presented throughout the second half of the book.

The pleasures that the successful seduction of women affords are great, and, like all good things in life, they don't come cheap (nor without responsibility—it almost goes without saying, but remember to be safe). But you've already taken the first step toward securing yourself more of them. Read on for some of the best advice, tips, wisdom, and secrets of success we've offered on our site, AskMen.com, on one of our favorite topics.

RULE 1: CONFIDENCE

There's a sea of dating doctors, love gurus, and pickup artists out there, all peddling their own techniques and strategies for landing successful women. And while the advice of these competing experts rarely overlaps, there's a near-unanimous consensus on the one crucial element required for success with women: Confidence. Confidence is the deal-maker and the deal-breaker, and if there's one fundamental rule in the game of love, it's that the first step toward intimacy with a woman is approaching her.

When it comes to approaching women, knowing exactly what to

expect is crucial—what may happen, why it happens, and how to over-come obstacles. The main reason so many men fail to approach and talk to women is because they fear the unknown such as the possible slap of rejection. Naturally, the more knowledge you have, the more confident you will be. You need to be ready at all times.

The truth of the matter is that you cannot depend on destiny or co-incidence to deliver you into romantic encounters. You must have the confidence to approach women, and if you don't, you must develop it.

USE CONFIDENCE TO PICK UP ANY WOMAN

Confidence is every man's number-one weapon in the game of seduc-tion.

However, it is one of the hardest character traits to fake, and also one of the most misunderstood. Part of the mystery behind confidence is that most men don't understand its nature. Some think that in order to emit confidence, one must show it through actions alone, while others believe confidence is acquired through words, and still others think one is born with it. There's also a common belief that confidence is something we can always control, but it is instead dependent on several factors—some of which we have no control over whatsoever.

If you want to master confidence and retain it for life, you must learn to incorporate, monitor, and balance six key elements within your daily routine. The moment you stop, everything can come crashing down with a comment as simple as "You're not my type."

Confidence breeds further confidence, and you will ultimately arrive at a frame of mind wherein your confidence feels like a natural part of your character; a trait that was always there. Arriving at this state, how-ever, will require persistence, fortitude, and patience. Let's start with the basics.

6 Key Elements to Help You Achieve Confidence

1. State of mind

The very first step toward becoming a confident person involves building internal confidence through daily introspection. You're going to have to help yourself by adopting a confidence-building philosophy.

What does this mean? By thinking about and creating exercises of confidence, your body will react and display that confidence. But before you can get there, you need to take a deep and honest look at yourself. You need to learn to feed off your strengths and eliminate—or at least minimize—your weaknesses. For example, if you think that stuttering when you're nervous is one weakness that contributes to your lack of confidence, then practice speaking with as many people (preferably women) as possible until you eliminate that drawback.

You need to develop personal habits that will put you into the right frame of mind and keep your confidence machine oiled and running strong. Try the following to keep yourself motivated:

Talk to yourself: Practice speaking in the morning before leaving the house by clearing your throat and saying aloud, "Good morning. You look damn good. You are number one." It may seem ridiculous and it may feel ridiculous, and you'll likely laugh at yourself over the first few efforts. But your self-consciousness will dissipate as you feel the effects of this positive reinforcement technique gradually take hold.

Keep a list of your strengths: Write down ten traits that will make you invaluable to any woman who's lucky enough to get your attention and time. (Get used to thinking this way about yourself.)

Change negative outlooks into positive ones: Stop being depressed about being single. Instead of worrying about being alone, be happy that you have the opportunity to meet a world of single women.

2. Physical appearance

Your physical appearance plays a very big role in your level of confidence. Not so much regarding how you feel about yourself, but how other people make you feel. Think back to those times when you put that extra effort into your appearance, and were rewarded with approving looks on the street. Now think about the jolt of confidence that those same looks gave you—imagine the effects of receiving them every day!

You should be exercising regularly, maintaining a healthy diet, and making all other requisite efforts in order to give the ladies what they like—a fit, healthy-looking, well-kept, and generally inviting appearance.

3. Your clothes

Your wardrobe obviously plays a significant role in maintaining an inviting appearance. Dress the part and you will fulfill it—the extra swagger in your step when you're dressed to the nines doesn't emerge out of nowhere. This doesn't mean that you need to make every occasion a black-tie affair, but when you do dress down, do so in a manner that remains stylish and flatters your physique and body type. You'll find plenty of assistance in this endeavor in the Fashion channel of AskMen.com.

4. Listening skills

Take a good look at any social situation, and you'll see that the man talking the most and the loudest is rarely the most confident one. When in a conversation with a woman, ration your words and prioritize listening to her. Encourage her to talk more by opening your mouth only to ask open-ended questions (for instance, asking what her favorite color is would be a definite no-no. More on this will follow in Chapter 2).

Handing off the bulk of the conversation to her in this manner will both conceal the nervousness you may be experiencing and give her occasion to focus the discussion on herself—which will ensure that she remembers the conversation as a pleasant one.

When you do respond, you don't need to make a congressional speech. Keep your contributions short and simple, especially when you first meet someone. The more you open your mouth, the greater the chance of saying something dumb, which, in turn, will cause you to get nervous, which will lead to a negative state of mind, which will lead to lower confidence, which leads to more nervousness, which leads to more stuttering . . . you get the picture.

5. Roll with the punches

Just because you're confident today, doesn't mean you will be forever, let alone tomorrow. Similarly, you may lose your confidence, but this doesn't mean you've lost it for good. It's important to manage your expectations with realistic outlooks. By doing so, it will be easier to rebound from harsh situations.

It is very easy to go from ultra-confidence to flat-out depression based on someone's comments—particularly those of a gorgeous woman. But no matter who you are, rejection will inevitably arise. The key is to not let it have a disproportionate effect on you. The great thing about the pickup game is that there will always be a next opportunity—there's no shortage of women out there. So if you get turned down, shake it off and move on to the next prospect.

6. Practice in the field

Improving your social skills will definitely have a large impact on your confidence. One long-term strategy to adopt in order to gradually build up social confidence is to resolve to smile at five people on a daily basis— and don't limit yourself to beautiful women. Eventually, you can add a friendly "hello," too. Get in the habit of being more amicable toward both women and men, regardless of their appearance.

After you've gotten into the habit of smiling and greeting people, you'll begin to feel comfortable enough to spark up small talk with friendly strangers in places like elevators or lines. Before you know it, you'll be making small talk with just about any woman who crosses your path.

After you've practiced the art of small talk for a while, you're going to discover something odd—confidence will become a part of your being! So keep it up. And if you ever encounter an anti-social individual who rudely ignores you, just remember Element No. 5 (Roll with the Punches), and don't worry about it.

Confident vs. Cocky

Before you run into the streets to flaunt your newfound self-assurance, be aware that there's a very fine line between confidence and cockiness. Make sure you know the difference and are smart enough to avoid the latter.

The difference between confidence and cockiness resides in the internal drive behind each. If you are naturally confident, it will effortlessly shine through in your demeanor. However, if you try to pretend to be confident through artificial inflation—by bragging about your car, your job, or how great a lover you are—you'll come off as cocky.

Remember: cockiness accomplishes the exact opposite of what confidence does—it's a turn-off to women.

TAKE CARE OF NO. 1

■ It's important to realize that the factor you have the most control over is yourself. Putting the entire emphasis on women will only lead you to make excuses about your interactions. Own your behavior.

■ Self-confidence comes from within. Don't slouch; stand up straight. Don't mumble; speak clearly. Portray an air of confidence. Simply put: If you believe you're the best, you'll become the best, and then women will believe you're the best too.

ALWAYS BE PREPARED FOR SEX

Earlier, we touched upon the idea of appearance breeding confidence. Let's revisit this notion in a bit more detail.

The right appearance is something of a self-fulfilling prophecy; dress the part and you will feel the part. It's the very same logic that underlies the art of the pickup: When you are physically and mentally prepared for romantic possibilities, you'll find that they come your way more easily.

Of course, you're not just maintaining a good appearance as a tool to elevate your confidence. There are women looking at you, and you want them to like what they see. The fact remains that women will always have more suitors than men and for this reason, women can afford to be a little pickier about the men they choose to play with. This is why it is so important that you prime yourself to be picked.

The competition out there is ferocious, and those who succeed in landing women are those who realize and provide women with what they want. And one basic thing that all women want is a man with proper hygiene.

■ When you look at yourself in the mirror, try to see yourself from the point of view of a woman who's attracted to you. Don't emphasize or dwell on the negative—like acne, or a receding hairline. If she's attracted to you, that's not what she's looking at. Instead, think of the compliments you've received in the past from women, and focus on those things.

■ Do the same as above for your personality. What have women complimented you on before, or at least responded favorably to? If it helps—and it probably will—write these things down. Seeing it on paper makes it more concrete to you, and less doubtable.

I. Grooming

Although women hate to admit it, upon first impression most of them judge a man based on his outward appearance. So the first step in seducing a woman is presenting her with an image that appeals to her.

Preparation tips:

Clothing: Every man's style is unique and his own to dictate, but there are certain maintenance tips that apply to all wardrobes. Your clothes should be clean—from the outermost layer to the innermost ones. Your clothes should be intact and wrinkle-free. And your clothes should be appropriate for your physique and body type. Assembling a wardrobe that fits this last bill is no simple feat; it will require time and plenty of trial and error. Your best starting point, again, is the Fashion channel at AskMen.com.

Nose hair / Eyebrows: Use scissors, tweezers, or special trimmers once a week to remove any unsightly hair from your nose, ears, and eyebrows.

Hair: Make sure that your hairstyle goes with the times and matches your clothing style as well as your age. Oh, and make sure it's grease- and dandruff-free. And if you're balding, the last thing you want to do is fall into the comb-over trap.

Teeth: Brush your teeth every morning and evening, floss your teeth before going to bed, and see your dentist every six months to have your teeth cleaned. Clean, white teeth are a sign of good health. Fresh breath is a sign of cleanliness and will make it a lot easier for you to socialize with the ladies.

Skin: Women are turned off by greasy, acne-covered skin. Wipe any excess grease from your skin regularly and wash your face before going to bed. A moisturizer will help keep your skin smooth and soft—it may seem unmanly, but these are qualities women love when it comes to a man's face.

Facial hair: A common belief, unfair though it may seem, is that men with facial hair have something to hide. Shave every day—especially before you go out on a date. However, there are a few men who look better with facial hair than without. If this is the case with you, then at least keep it short, well-trimmed, and, for God's sake, food-free.

Odor: If you're going to reveal your body to a beautiful woman, you'll be revealing the smell of your body to her as well. You *must* control your odor. It's no secret that women love fresh scents. So shower on a daily basis, use deodorant, and apply some cologne where appropriate (without going overboard—the point is to smell nice, not draw unnecessary attention).

II. Mental Preparation

You look the part, and you've ensured that she won't encounter any embarrassing blemishes or odors. Your state of mind will benefit from your carefully groomed appearance, but you will have to take additional steps to prep a truly winning attitude.

Preparation tips:

Charm: Charm is not a single characteristic that can be easily adopted; it is perhaps better defined as a collection of traits that work together to create an intangible yet compelling attractiveness. It is no more easily assumed than it is defined, but one can take steps toward projecting charm in a very concrete fashion. Here are some points to start you off:

■ Eye contact is charm's ally. Never forget to look into a woman's eyes when speaking to her.

■ Compliment her. What you should compliment is relatively easy; just figure out what it would take to make you feel grateful and do the same to others. Make sure your compliments always emerge from a sincere place. The difference between charm and flattery is that flattery has an agenda (i.e., I'll flatter you so that you'll give me what I want). Charm is a way of being, rather than a means to achieve something.

Humor: Laughter is the best icebreaker for when you first approach a woman. A sense of humor is one of the top turn-ons for many women. A positive and friendly attitude toward life in general will help you be naturally happy and more pleasant to be around.

Brains: Women like to know that there is more to you than two nuts between your legs and air between your ears. That's why it is important to have a broad general knowledge. Read up on current events constantly, and make the effort to populate your to-read list with books on diverse topics—tackle one a month.

HOW TO PICK UP WOMEN
ACCORDING TO YOUR LOOKS

Independent measures can go a long way toward instilling confidence in oneself. Nevertheless, you may feel that your confidence is limited by something outside of your control: your looks.

Got a big nose, a little gut, a below-average-sized penis? Remember that women don't consider men's physical appearance to be nearly as important as men do women's. In fact, attributes like looks typically rank below confidence, sense of humor, and compassion when it comes to the men that women choose.

That being said, physical shortcomings will still likely have an effect on your psyche, and can inhibit you even if they shouldn't. You need to counter them by proving to yourself that they needn't have an effect on your success rate.

You can't head straight to the hottest woman in the room and get to work. Rejection stings and makes you even shyer than when you got to the club in the first place. No, you need to practice your technique and build your level of confidence before you can approach any woman with a good chance that you will not only leave with her that evening, but also have her screaming your name so loud and so often that she will never forget it (we'll tell you how you're going to do that later).

Read on to start understanding your level of physical appeal, how to pick up according to your level, and modifying your other personality traits so that you can move on up to the intimidating beauties that you want.

And always remember: regardless of your looks, Rule Number One is confidence.

Start Off in Your Range

Remember, an exceptional woman has *options*.

A beautiful, successful, intelligent woman—a 9 or a 10 on a scale of attractiveness—is probably approached by men (either overtly or just by way of innocent flirting during conversation) an average of four or five times *a day*. That's a lot of competition. And for a woman who is approached so often, there would be no way to spend time with many (or any) of these suitors even if she *wanted* to. She doesn't have the time or the energy, so she has to weed guys out quickly, based on very little information—a nerve-racking situation for you.

You need to accept the fact that in the dating game, people are constantly raising red or green flags internally, based on the current interaction. Hell, you do it, right? So in order to get some positive reinforcement, which is nowhere more important than in dating—where *who you are* is being judged—you should start off with someone more in your range. She'll be happy about the attention and will give you the time of day (and night, you hope), giving you more opportunities for a successful interaction.

If you consider yourself to be a 5, go after a 5, to start. If you consider yourself to be a 1, 2, 3, or 4, you should still start off with what you perceive to be a 5. A guy's gotta have motivation, right? Chances are, you won't be as nervous around a girl whose looks are equal to or only slightly better than yours. That's because she'll be less choosy, and will give you more leeway.

Boost Your Confidence

Slowly, you'll learn that talking to women is not that intimidating. Perfect your pickup technique on the 5s before you move on to greener pastures.

If a 5 shoots you down, that's fine, move on to the next 5 and the next (you may have noticed that there are lots of 5s out there to practice on), until you alter your technique and improve it.

Take Them to Bed

Your practice work with the 5s won't end at the pickup. Don't be cocky, but do maintain the confidence that helped you get the woman into bed once you're in the sack together. Once you manage to seduce a 5, say, take her to bed and take your time. Take advantage of the opportunity to experiment. You can practice all sorts of things and really hone your technique with a woman who's happy about getting the attention.

See your average-looking partners a number of times. You can learn plenty more about general sexual techniques once you're used to a woman's sensitive points (all women are a little different), and once she feels comfortable with you and therefore less inhibited, she'll even give you feedback (which you could and should ask for)—the most useful sexual ammunition you'll get, and a major confidence-booster for future conquests.

To elicit this kind of feedback, don't ask general questions like "How am I doing?" or "Is this any good?" That sounds needy and insecure, like you're simply fishing for compliments. Instead, be specific and take the emphasis off yourself, which from her perspective takes your ego out of the equation. For example, say, "Do you prefer when I rub your clitoris like this . . . or like this?" or "Which position feels best, like this . . . or like this?" She may choose neither of the two options, but you opened the door for her to tell you how she really likes it.

Once you master that technique, you can branch out and alter it a little, based on what other lovers have liked and what *you* like. Often, you'll end up teaching her something. Also, asking not only makes the sex more physically stimulating, it also shows her you've got her interests in mind (which, of course, you do), which scores you huge points with her and earns you future play dates—to practice even more.

Move Up in Rank

Now that you've seduced and conquered the women at your level and improved your sexual technique in so doing, it's time to move up the scale to, say, a 7 or an 8. Start the process all over again. This time, it likely won't take as long, considering your confidence is noticeably higher and therefore making you more appealing to the ladies. You may find yourself moving up quite quickly, but don't aim too high too fast or you may set yourself up for a fall.

Keep in mind that if you're happy with someone at your level of physical appeal, or even below it, then stick with it. Sometimes the 5s are wilder in bed and will impress you intellectually—there's no correlation between looks and intelligence. Between looks and attitude? Definitely. In general, average-looking women are certainly more down to earth. But if all you want is to tap the 10s—to at least know what it's like, if not to find a keeper—then carry on up that way.

You won't need to seek out any evidence of your increased confidence; you'll feel it resonate throughout your character. More importantly, your increased self-assuredness will shine through in all manner of day-to-day activities, and everyone from your friends to your coworkers to your romantic targets will pick up on it.

Yet, while the rewards of confidence aren't restricted to the dating game, the focus of this book is. So let's not lose sight of our goals here. You've now got the confidence to approach women; it's time to address what you're going to do—or, rather, what you're going to say—upon your face-to-face arrival.

RULE 2: CONVERSATION

You've optimized your sense of confidence, and you've accustomed yourself to approaching complete strangers with an eye toward chatting. You've also learned what a powerful tool listening is in conversation, but that won't entirely exclude you from talking. When you do open your mouth, how can you overcome residual nerves and avoid coming off like a babbling idiot?

The answer is simple: practice. The more you speak to women, and, even more importantly, listen to them, the more natural you'll be when you're caught off-guard, and the more easily you'll be able to direct the conversation (and the encounter) in the most satisfying possible direction.

HOW TO MAKE SMALL TALK

Forget about having a whole conversation with someone; the thought of making small talk, whether it's with a date, coworker, or stranger, makes your palms sweat (in which case you want to avoid shaking the person's hand at all costs). You're not alone: Even seasoned conversationalists dread the perceived artificiality of small talk.

Yet however artificial small talk may seem, it's a necessary evil. After all, you've got to talk about something, right? And small talk can lead to big talk, which can lead to big dates, big opportunities, and generally good things. So the next time you dismiss a small-talk opportunity, just think about all the possibilities this eliminates.

Using these tips, making small talk with a woman will no longer feel like pulling teeth, and you will do so more efficiently—that's to say, in a direction toward a more substantial conversation.

Ask a Lot of Questions

Asking questions provides a basis of good conversation, helps you get to know the woman you're talking with, and gives her occasion to talk about herself—which all women love. Don't just throw any question out there, however; asking her what her favorite color is neither reflects well on your mental capacity, nor does it open the door to an extended discussion. Your question should be open-ended in the sense that it paves the way for further conversation, whether in the form of a debate (conducted in a playful and light-hearted manner, of course), further questioning, or expansion into additional topics.

Questions also show that you have a genuine interest in her, as long as you show her that you also listen to her responses (she may quiz you later).

Talk About Casual Topics

First-date conversation topics can be a book unto itself, but in a nutshell, keep the conversation light, interesting, and free of anything philosophical, sexual, or personal. Steer clear of discussing her work—it may conjure up negative connotations, and falling on such a clichéd topic points to a lack of imagination. Launching into a discussion about her family or yours may be perceived as too forward or personal.

You can't go wrong by being casual. Talk about how good or bad the music is. Employ the environment, and tie in its elements with a funny anecdote. Make a remark about how great your drink is, and tell her how it's made (you'll have learned with an eye toward ordering it beforehand). Make a general comment about the situation you're in, and steer this general topical starting point to a more specific one.

Mix It Up

Don't be afraid to throw a random remark into the mix; for the woman who's courted frequently, hearing the unexpected can be refreshing. A remark doesn't have to be controversial or completely out of left field to be "random"; you don't want her to dismiss you as a wacko. Use your surroundings to point out something of curiosity, or ask her opinion on a topic that may seem tangential but that you can navigate toward a more significant discussion. Another route is to declare your unique perspective on common topic, inspiring her to declare her own opinion and take the discussion to a new level. As long as you avoid anything too personal or potentially controversial, and know which questions to ask, you'll be talking the talk and walking the walk . . . of a certified schmoozer.

Q: What's the phone call protocol? How many times should I try before I leave a message? How many times before I give up entirely?

A: Never leave a message on the first attempt. You'll be caught off guard at having to do so, and it will shine through in your voice. Consider that your call for the day, and save your second—and final—attempt for the next day.

If her machine picks up on your second attempt, you're faced with the tricky part: what to say. Whenever possible, make your message short, sweet, and to the point. The longer you speak, the more likely you are to lose your cool. Leave a simple and polite message with your name and your digits, then get out while the getting's good.

Ideally, she will get back to you in the next two days, but don't be concerned if she doesn't. She could be away, swamped with work, or involved in a personal or family crisis. If she doesn't respond after four days, she's either not interested or she's trapped at the bottom of a well. Either way, you're better off moving on.

THE PICKUP: GOOD & BAD CONVERSATION TOPICS

You can't enjoy a conversation with a beautiful woman without initiating it, and you can't initiate it without approaching her. If you think that you can wait for *her* to make the approach, you're mistaken. Not because there's no such chance, but because the onus is on you, the man, to make the approach. There's no use debating the fairness of it; it's just the way it is.

So how do you go about crossing that massive, intimidating gulf separating you from the object of your interest? The key is to be quick, firm, and decisive. Don't stand around and dwell on it—doing so will only allow doubts to seep into your mind and shake your confidence, and the sight of you lurking and staring nervously from the corner certainly isn't going to elevate your chances with her. If anything, it's going to freak her out.

So spring to action. Once you make that decision to approach, execute. Straighten your back, broaden your shoulders out, take a breath, and let that confidence you've been building up swell throughout your body. Fix your eyes on her, get yourself next to her, and strike up your pickup conversation.

In many ways, picking up women is just a numbers game; instances of success will usually be outnumbered by instances of failure. That's the simple reality, and it shouldn't stop your from persisting in spotting and approaching women.

Yet nor should you use "the numbers game" as an excuse. If you're getting turned down in short order by women who *should* be receptive—women who are all dolled up and looking lonely in a bar or club, for example—then it's time to realize it's not them, it's you. You're doing something wrong, and wasting your time and hurting your ego in the process. We know that the problem doesn't reside in your confidence, your appearance, or your small talk skills (right?); what needs adjusting is your pickup conversation.

There are really two very different and important aspects to a conversation with the specific goal of picking up. They are:

1. The How

2. The What

The How

Most guys want to know "what to talk about" with women. Well, it only makes sense that you should talk about things that women are interested in, right? For example, NASCAR stats and power tools are obviously not your best way in.

But it is actually much more important that you talk about any topic in the *right way*. In other words, if you don't understand *how* to carry on a conversation that creates attraction, then it really won't matter *what* you talk about. You won't trigger attraction in the woman, and so, try as you might, she'll never feel anything toward you.

Think about it this way: let's say you learn from a friend of your pickup target that her passion is the environment. You then strike up a conversation about the environment—how no one is paying enough attention to it, how the world is going to hell in a hand basket, etc.

Right buttons, should work, right? Not if you go about it the wrong way—you don't make eye contact, you never make jokes, you don't listen to her, you're only negative, etc. How's that going to go over? Like a lead balloon.

The *how* of pickup conversation includes (but is not limited to):

■ Using your body language: Show self-confidence by sitting up straight or standing tall, and looking relaxed (e.g., not fidgeting).

■ Making eye contact: Remember, look her in the eye when you talk, and especially when you listen.

■ Learning how to say things in a way that clearly communicates that you don't need her to like you or approve of you. Make her laugh, but move on quickly to the next topic instead of reveling in the fact you've made her laugh. When you can make a woman laugh while *not* seeking her approval, you have a powerful combination that sparks attraction.

Basically, if you're getting a lot of "uncomfortable silences," nervousness, and other normal challenges for a beginner, you probably need to get the how handled before the what.

FLIRTING TIPS

■ Keep it light: You can talk about serious subjects, but insert a positive spin on them now and then to show you're not a downer or depressive.

■ Use humor: Don't feel the need to be funny constantly, like a clown, but know that women do rank a man's ability to make them laugh as very important.

■ Direct the conversation: Don't monopolize it, but do bring in new topics rather than just letting her steer you around like a water-ski boat driver. Wives may like to feel they can control their men, but pickups don't.

■ Use compliments appropriately: Don't overdo it.

■ Be talkative: Be ready and able to converse briefly about common questions and topics.

■ Don't seek her approval: This one is very important. Whether for casual play or the long term, women want a guy who is a challenge. Needy, weak personalities aren't generally perceived as attractive ones, and, furthermore, women like the ego-boost of landing the elusive target . . . just like men do.

The What

What are good topics to discuss with women?

Here's a hint: What topics do women pay to hear about? In other words, what are the topics that dominate female media—women's magazines, romance novels, soap operas, and nighttime dramas? For whatever reason, women tend to love:

■ Drama

■ Conflict

■ Romance

■ Famous people and their lives

■ Psychology

Familiarize yourself with these topics so that you'll be able to make interesting conversation about them. These days, we're so bombarded with infotainment that you'd have to make a special effort to avoid it.

If you catch a few minutes of an entertainment news show before you head out, read a few headlines on supermarket tabloids and magazines while you wait, and read the odd article in a tabloid–style newspaper about a tragic fire, arrest, or other personal news story, you're good to go.

On the other hand, it won't help you at all to bring up these topics if you can't actually carry on a conversation about them. Then your strategy to *try* to seem interesting will be laid bare, which looks bad.

Be sure to feel her out during your conversation. For example, if she's a lawyer, she might not have much time to watch TV and discuss shows, but instead she knows more about high-profile court cases going on.

Topics to avoid: Kidnapping, stalking, death, chess, computers, comic books, *Star Wars*, *Star Trek*, your secret love for wrestling, mixed martial arts. Put yourself in her shoes and never talk about topics that might really freak a woman out. You'll create bad vibes that will make any attraction that you've created instantly disappear.

Don't talk negatively about yourself or your friends. It shows you're needy or don't really care for those who are close to you. If you think that about yourself or your friends, what do you think of her?

Avoid looking desperate. Don't talk about how desperate you are or how long it's been since you've been on a date.

Don't fish for her approval by asking if she likes you or if you're her "type," constantly asking her things like "Are you having fun?" and "Are you okay?" Basically, steer clear of any topic that makes you look insecure and needy.

The beauty of pickup conversations lies in ample opportunity to practice them. So get out there and turn the "numbers game" into a game of getting numbers.

TOP 5 TOPICS TO AVOID

1. Your Vices

Why it's taboo: Treat your first few dates with a woman as you would a job interview—you wouldn't want her to find out anything about you that would make you seem unreliable in the long run.

2. Money

Why it's taboo: The motto when it comes to money is "show, don't tell." Talking about any financial issues with a woman early on is considered tacky.

3. Past Conquests

Why it's taboo: You might think that if she knows you are a man in demand, you will be more desirable. However, telling her about your past dating experiences is not only boring for her, but it also makes you sound like a player.

4. Your Ailments

Why it's taboo: If the only thing you can come up with is that you have a knee, wrist, or hip problem, you really need to brush up on your conversational skills.

5. Your Future as a Couple

Why it's taboo: Yes, women generally want men that are serious minded and thinking about the future. But they don't want crazy and clingy men either.

TOP 5 THINGS TO DISCUSS

The trick to successful chitchat is to keep the conversation smooth, and avoid those dreaded silences where your nervous urge to fill the gaps makes you blurt out something you wished you hadn't.

Again, keep the questions coming—not like an interview, but rather like you're chatting with your pals.

1. Traveled Anywhere Special?

A tricky way to spark a girl's interest is by asking about past travel destinations and where she intends to visit in the future. This also provides both people with some insight into each other's cultural background and their openness to new adventures.

2. Pop Culture

Talk about the shows you find most fascinating. A word of warning: don't talk as if TV is the center of your existence. It's hard to seem interesting when your life centers around the tube.

HOW TO DISARM WOMEN DURING A PICKUP

Have you ever noticed how a woman not interested in you (for example, a happily married woman) has no problem interacting with you breezily and confidently, whereas a woman who ultimately turned out to be interested was a much tougher nut to crack?

That's because the interested woman sees you as a potential mate, and wants to put you through tests to see if you're worthy. And someone putting you through tests will automatically be much more on her guard, as she's preparing, if you pass, to put herself in a vulnerable position with you.

So *how* can you get her to let her guard down, the better to penetrate her inner sanctum of happiness and become part of it (even if just for one night)?

3. Her Friends

Her girlfriends are her pillars of support and cohorts in good times. Ask her about them, how she met them, where they go together. This is when you get precious details about her.

4. Future Plans

She'll love it if you ask her about her goals, dreams, and ambitions. Ask her about her ideal job, where she'd like to live, who she'd like to emulate, and how she plans on making it all happen. But don't attempt to integrate yourself into those plans, or make transparent attempts to align them with your own. Overeager commitment can be just as unattractive to women as it is to men.

5. What She Does for Fun

To gauge her tastes (and for a hint about where you should take her on a date), ask her where she likes to go on weekends, what activities she prefers, and if she's a social butterfly or a lone ranger. Ask her if she likes sports, and if so, ask her which ones she practices.

Read on to find out what to do, and what not to do, to get a woman feeling more relaxed around you while you chat her up.

Get Her Opinion

While chatting, don't simply talk about current events, for example, without delving deeper. How does she *feel* about what you're talking about? You can start out with something simple like favorite movie stars, but do try to elicit her opinions. "Why do you think he just left her like that?" "Do you think he did the right thing?" Sometimes ask her opinion before divulging yours (or she might just parrot you), but not always, or it will become formulaic ("What do you think about this?" "What about that?" etc.) and she will feel compromised, in that she's always stating her position without knowing yours, making her vulnerable.

Eliciting her opinion serves several purposes:

1. It shows you really care what she thinks.

2. Whether you agree or disagree, you can turn it to your advantage. If you agree: you have something in common, and can talk further on the subject. If you disagree: you can start playfully teasing her about her opinion. Teasing leads the way to sexual teasing and innuendo, which spices things up.

Try to agree more at first, to make her feel an affinity with you. Once you've established a little common ground, you can start to disagree more (cue teasing). Never disagree with everything she says, no matter what your opinion, or you'll seem like a jerk. Agree too much, however, and she'll see you either as her soul mate (if she's searching for one) or spineless (if she's on the prowl like you).

If a woman is very reluctant to divulge her opinions, it may well be a sign that either a) she is not interested in you, or b) she is boring. Neither is good, so move on.

Make Her Laugh

This is the ultimate weapon. If you can make a woman laugh, you're more than halfway home. Laughter loosens up conversation and the overall pickup. The thing is, it has to be natural, not planned. Women's No. 1 turn-on is confidence, and approaching with a pat pickup line or joke means you're resorting to a formula. Don't try to force humor or fall back on controversial topics—political and gender-based jokes will definitely inspire a reaction, but not the one you're looking for. Sincere humor is largely universal; be true to what makes you laugh, and you'll inspire her to do the same.

Bring Her to a Happy Place & Stay Positive

Maybe you're not the funniest guy in the world. There are still other ways to rub her conversational belly without necessarily bringing her to tears of laughter. Make her feel positive by talking about happy subjects—vacation, for example. She's either been on one recently and can tell you about that, or will be going soon and is excited with anticipation. Either way, it's a more positive subject than famine, right?

It doesn't have to be only fluffy subjects, though. You can talk about politics, if that's what she's into, but make light of it along the way, ridiculing people as you see fit or, even safer, the system in general. If you can show a woman that you can see the lighter side of any issue, you then become her chaperone to light-hearted times.

Give Her an Original Compliment

Tell a girl she has nice eyes when she doesn't and it will seem so mechanical, you might as well insult her. On the other hand, try to steer clear of obvious compliments. You'll get a lot more bang from a compliment she hasn't heard before. Compliment her belt, watch, shoes—whatever. The goal is to get her to crack a smile.

The key, obviously, is to be observant. Visual observations can go over extremely well—when used properly. Instead of "You have nice lips," try saying something like "Your lips are such a great shape. Good proportion, bottom lip just the right amount of pouty, but not so pouty that I could sit on it . . . Your whole lip/lipstick combination, it really works." A confident, tongue-in-cheek delivery is important.

Complimenting her ensemble is a good move because you can point out that it's well put together (to her credit), and also that it looks good on her (which is to her credit, in that she knows what flatters her, and also a straight up "you're hot" compliment). This makes her feel noticed and appreciated, so that she'll feel less insecure and will relax more.

Rather than giving many little compliments, try to use one solid, original showstopper. Look misty-eyed and distracted, as if mesmerized by what you're about to compliment. This will effectively "stop the show."

Use Negative Hits

What is a negative hit? Think of it as a playful, lighthearted insult or tease, delivered to the beautiful woman in lieu of the clichéd compliment she usually hears. In other words, it's the last thing she expects to hear, but the one thing she'll remember at the end of the night. If you fawn all over her and never give her a dose of reality, she will quickly grow tired of your overly positive, wolf-crying chatter. Hot women don't need another fan club; they need a challenge. Breaking up conversation with the odd negative hit or tease (adapted to her personality, of course) will tell her she can also speak her mind freely. Then, watch the sparks fly.

THE NEGATIVE HIT

Nothing in the content or the delivery of a negative hit should be mean-spirited. The negative hit is playful and often tongue-in-cheek in tone, but nevertheless always pointed in its goal: To gently shake its female subject's confidence and arouse her curiosity in the process. As a woman receives compliments over the course of an evening, they lose their value and significance. In this context, negative hits become all the more effective by contrast.

Tell a woman that she has beautiful eyes, and she's likely to roll them. Wryly deliver the seemingly innocuous remark, "You have something in your eye," and you'll simultaneously disorient her, pique her curiosity, and distinguish yourself from all the guys who tried to suck up to her before you. As you become accustomed to rolling out negative hits, you can become bolder with them. "Those shoes look comfortable" is a very loaded comment to a female's ears, and one that will definitely set you apart from the rest of the pack.

Don't Talk About Sex Right Away

Let her get comfortable with you before you introduce the subject. And when you do bring it up, it should obviously be in a joking way.

Don't Jump to Conclusions

Nothing makes a person clam up faster than if they feel they've been pigeonholed. Let's say you give her the up and down and, based on her low-cut jeans and bellybutton ring, ask her out of the blue what she thinks of the latest teenage popstar's album. She'll either think you obviously take her for a fan based on her attire, or else, if she has low self-esteem, she may feel silly for not having an opinion.

Never assume, always ask. If you want to bring up this subject, sidle up to it, or just ask her what her musical interests are. Then, when you do bring it up, it will seem more like it's also your interest (which she may indeed share) than something you've projected onto her.

In the end, study all these ideas beforehand—rather than overthinking them on the fly—then just be your charming self. Remember: you have to be confident and natural if you want a woman to be drawn to you.

BE SUGGESTIVE WITHOUT BEING LEWD

A good part of effective conversation technique is clearly communicating your intents. And when your intents aren't entirely honorable, in the more traditional sense, communication can be awkward. One of the hardest things for any guy to do is make the transition from flirting in the bar to grooving in the bedroom. Unless the stars are aligned and everything just falls into place (i.e., she whispers in your ear how much she wants to do you), you are going to have to work hard to make it

Q: I'm looking to make a great impression on a first date. Where are some good places to go?

A: First-date locations have a lot to do with personal taste, but certain stand-bys are guaranteed to get your encounter off on the right foot. For starters, try to focus on places that will promote conversation and give you a chance to get to know one another. This means abandoning movies and plays, for example, in favor of a trip to your local art gallery. Granted, you might not know which way to hang a Picasso, but your date will appreciate your inner culture vulture. If you prefer a more outdoorsy setting, you can't go wrong with either zoos or amusement parks. Both will provide you with plenty of eye candy and entertainment in case your conversation hits a lull.

Sporting activities can also be fun and inexpensive. A night of bowling or an afternoon at the skating rink is a surefire bet. Just make sure to reign in your competitive impulses. Even if you're a former NHL prospect, your date will find it endearing if she has to pick you up from the ice on at least a couple of occasions.

Above all else, be flexible. If your date turns out to be a vegetarian, don't take her for ribs at Bloody Bob's Steakhouse just because that was the plan. No matter what the scenario, make sure to have a backup restaurant or café in mind in case your first choice turns out to be a dud.

---

happen. So, here are eight ways to give her a clear signal of your intentions without being crass.

1. Touch Her Casually

If you pull this off, your contact will be electric and get both of your motors running. We're not talking about shameless ass-grabbing or thigh-groping here. Focus on light, casual contact that naturally happens over the course of the night. Touch her arm while laughing at her jokes or gently guide her through a door by touching the small of her back.

2. Be Forthright Without Being Rude

Judge her mood, and if she seems open to it, tell her what you want to do to her. Don't use words like "plow" or "savage," but use passionate words whispered close to her ear. Tell her how crazy she is driving you and how you can't help yourself. Let her know how badly you want to put your hands on her. If she is still listening, you are in for a night to remember. Of course, she might end up pouring her drink on you, so be wary if you're wearing that $200 shirt.

3. Make Light of Your Intentions

It doesn't have to be all awkward and serious. You both know you want to get her home and shag her proper, but it is like a huge pink elephant in the middle of the club that neither of you is talking about. Have fun with this: Tell her you'll have to stop drinking or you might really disappoint her later, or ask her to rate your game out of 10. It isn't necessarily the number you are looking for, but the way she answers. A genuine laugh and smile mean you can ramp it up a bit. An awkward response means you have a lot of work to do.

4. Be Playful

This does not mean snapping her bra or tugging on her pigtails—leave that stuff for recess. But show her you are out to have a good time without being serious. Get on the dance floor, hit the mechanical bull, or challenge her to some good ol'-fashioned arm wrestling—anything that shows her you aren't just a serious player out to get some. She'll lighten up considerably and make your transition that much easier.

5. Suggest a Sinful, Albeit Nonsexual, Activity

One vice leads to another, so why not hit up the casino? The electric atmosphere and smell of money will act like a natural aphrodisiac, and you might get lucky in more ways than one.

You can also establish your street cred by suggesting an after-hours club. You can keep the party going longer, and the more Mai Tais she drinks, the more her inhibitions will fade away.

6. Get Bumping and Grinding

The electric energy of the dance floor, the pounding beat of the music, all those swaying, sweaty bodies in a kinetic pool of sexuality—oh man.

Proper grinding is an art form; do it too hard and she'll be grossed out immediately. Show a bit of restraint and subtly grind into her, and she will get the message loud and clear. It's a bit of a cliché, but only because it is such an effective way to segue from the club to the bedroom.

7. Give Her a Foot Rub

She's been dancing all night and her feet are sore. Grab a booth, buy her a drink and give her a thorough foot rub under the table. Let your hands wander ever so subtly upward, but not past the knee. She'll get an idea of your real intentions pretty quickly (while enjoying the foot rub, because who doesn't love one?).

8. Grab a Bite to Eat

Food is an undeniably effective aphrodisiac. So, get her out of the bar and into a nice little comfy booth where you can share some food. It's tactile, it's sensuous, and it lets you put things into her mouth. That's what you really want, isn't it?

LISTEN RIGHT FOR SEX THAT NIGHT

We can't emphasize this point enough: When it comes to conversation, the big difference between the big players of this world and the regular guys is their listening skills. Let's wrap up our chapter on conversation with a final primer on listening properly and responding to her dialogue.

Listen With Your Ears, Not Your Mouth

In general, most men are admittedly awful listeners, and they tend to talk too much. Most fellows take the listening approach secretly known as the "Feigning listening to her problems so that she can appreciate you more and want to have more sex with you." Such an approach, obviously, is the wrong one.

Nor, however, should you be too engaging in your listening. Your conversational partner already has her mommy, daddy, and her friends criticizing and lecturing her with their own moral advice. The last thing she wants is to meet yet another person who will foist their opinion on her about a particular problem.

She wants to meet someone who will listen and understand her, as well as relate to her problems without judgment or advice. In order to be this person, you have to chat using an "Active Listening Approach."

Be an Active Listener

It's not that hard to be an active listener, but it does require a few traits that men sometimes find elusive: patience, concentration, and modesty.

It requires patience because you have to give her as much time to listen to her message as she needs. Concentration is key because you have to not only look at her, but also focus on her: her eyes, her body language and her voice. What is she saying? What is she telling you? Concentrate.

Modesty is included here because a lot of men have a problem letting someone take the floor for an extended period of time. They like to hear their own voice and want others to hear it too. These men want to dominate the conversation and hold court, so to speak. This is not, sad to say, a trait conducive to good relationship rapport.

So toss your ego aside and let her speak. And above all else, let her have the last word once in a while. Hint: It's not a sign of masculine weakness to do so.

Your Active Style

Active listening skills are helpful in intelligence gathering. This skill is used to scan for hooks (points of interest to feed on) and red flags (subjects to avoid).

Here's how you can get started:

■ Encourage thoughts by asking her open-ended questions and then begin with your "active listening" skills.

■ Use minimal verbal encouragers such as "Yes, go on," "Okay," "I see," and "Uh huh."

■ Whenever she pauses, repeat the last few words of her last sentence and then pause.

■ Don't interrupt her and try to encourage her train of thought without agreeing or disagreeing. This will help you learn more about her.

■ Demonstrate your understanding as if you're walking in her stilettos.

■ Label her emotions in order to be perceived as empathetic (e.g., "You sound excited," "You sound tormented," "Wow, you're really passionate about . . ." or "I've never met someone so fervent about this").

■ Summarize her key points in your own words and pay special attention to the labeled emotions in order to demonstrate understanding and build trust (e.g., "Let me get this straight, you've been trying to get this job for over six months now and you finally got it today? I can understand why you're so excited about it.")

■ Be brief and identify with her by pointing out a common interest or feeling. If you listened well, you should have a few hooks to help you.

■ Steer the conversation toward gratification. Do not talk about sex, although it *is* okay to hint at it using stand-in distractions such as dessert, cars, clothing, vacations, celebrations, or drinks.

DO *NOT* BE ONE OF THESE GUYS:

The Pretender: This is the man who has the appearances of an active listener but at the end of the day does not give a damn about what his conversation partner has to say.

The Stage Hog: This is the guy who has to have all the attention, all the time. He loves to hear the sound of his own voice, to the detriment of prospective relationships. Whenever possible, he shifts the focus of the conversation to himself. Do not be this guy.

The Contradictor: Whether because he's consistently keen to get his point across or because he thrives on playing the devil's advocate, this guy is always introducing conflict to discussions. As aforementioned, you don't want to roll over and agree with everything a woman says, but nor should you always create debate for debate's sake.

Focus on Her Nonverbal Communication

It doesn't take that much to recognize when a woman is sad, upset, or angry. And if you're not as quick to respond, you'll be perceived either as a jerk who doesn't care and does it on purpose, or oblivious to the nuances of nonverbal communication.

Nonverbal communication includes gestures, movements, facial expressions, and other physical forms of body language. Take note, however: it also includes tone of voice, sighs, and vocal pitch and volume. Pay attention to all of these whenever you communicate with a woman.

In good and bad times, nonverbal communication will serve as an instant sign as to how she feels about you at that very moment, not to mention how she feels in general. No matter what words she chooses, her body language cannot mask her real emotions.

Know Your Tongue

Most women appreciate a man who knows how to actively listen without judging or providing too much advice. They love it when a man understands and validates their point (even if they're totally wrong). So if you want to get a woman on her backside, first you have to get on her good side by giving her the gift of an empathetic ear.

One more piece of advice before you open your ears: try not to drink and chat because alcohol will definitely influence your ability to communicate and listen properly. Although it's okay to have a few drinks to help you relax, you must never abuse your liquor. Remember: the more you drink, the more talking the bottle will do for you.

RULE 3: LEAVE HER WANTING MORE

Our first pickup rule addressed a personality trait which all dating experts acknowledge as a universal prerequisite for success with women: Confidence. Our third and present rule will focus on a general strategy that all dating experts acknowledge as an effective one. Some have called it "Being a Challenge," others call it "The Cat on the String Theory," while still others simply illustrate it using the old show biz adage "Leave them Wanting More." They all boil down to the same core notion: The more you withhold of yourself, the more of you she'll want.

Date Your Way to Sex

As the saying goes, good things come to those who wait. So take your time getting to know a woman, and letting her get to know you. A good first date doesn't necessarily have to end with cooking her breakfast.

Women love a mysterious man they can unravel, layer by layer, like the skin of an onion. If there is nothing left to discover, a woman might lose interest, but if she can see that there is much more to be revealed, she'll keep coming back.

If you prep properly for any awkward situations that might arise and pull off the fine balancing act between interested and indifferent, she'll never stop begging for more.

THE MYSTERY OF SILENCE

Most men feel very pressed for time, as if they only have a small window of opportunity to attract the attention of a woman. As a result, they feel that the only way to impress a woman is by telling her *everything* about themselves within the first few dates. Some men even go as far as telling their whole life story within the initial ten minutes of their first date.

Offering a woman too much information is the equivalent of revealing all your cards, without giving her the chance to develop an attraction for you. Also, there is a danger here that she might discover some flaws in your character, and a woman is less forgiving when her interest level is not yet fully established. It will be a lot easier for a woman to drop you during the initial stages of the relationship, when she still hasn't invested too much time in you, or fallen for you blindly.

Additionally, because of this small window of opportunity, men feel that the best way to sell themselves is by impressing women with materialistic sales pitches. *Talking only about themselves* really means what they own, the type of car they drive, how fast the car can go from 0 to 60 mph, how much money they make, and so on.

This is a big mistake, and will only result in scaring women away. During the initial encounter or the first few dates, women hate to hear men brag about their accomplishments or the assets they own.

Sure, women are impressed, but they would rather find out about your "assets" on their own and not through your car salesman pitch. For women, one of the biggest turn-offs is a man who cannot stop talking about himself.

Mystery Is an Asset

So how do you stay mysterious? Well you can start by following these four basic rules:

1. Conduct the interview

You're not giving your cards away and you're remaining mysterious as long as she keeps talking. By asking all the questions, she will feel like she has to prove her worthiness to you.

2. Never blab about the past

Keep the past in the past. Don't bring up your ex during a conversation, mention how hurt you were, or talk about the fiancée who left you.

3. Your family does not exist

Don't talk about your gay uncle, your sister's ten children, your mother's drinking habit, or your father's gambling addiction. Your date is not a therapist and does not need to hear about your family problems. At least not yet.

4. No specifics

It's okay to talk about your job. She will definitely talk about it or bring it up, but don't talk about how much money you make.

The Moral of the Story

Okay, you can't stay mysterious for the rest of your life, or the mystery may only serve to scare her away. Eventually, you will have to divulge a little more information about yourself. Just don't do it during the first couple of dates.

Q: How many dates in can I stop paying for everything?

A: It's been said that money is the root of all evil. That's especially true in the realm of dating, where finances—or a lack thereof—have ruined many new relationships. Unfortunately for you, the equality of the sexes generally doesn't extend to the first few weeks of dating.

The general rule of thumb is that the person who has arranged the date should also be responsible for paying. Let's face it, though: Unless you want to be mistaken for Scrooge, it's a wise idea to pick up the tab for your first three or four excursions. By this point, it is generally understood that you are past the courting stage, and you should be comfortable enough with one another to split expenses. For instance, if you buy dinner, she should pick up the movie tickets. And if you pay for the first three drinks at the strip club, she should pick up the final lap dance.

HOW TO KEEP HER ON HER TOES

In the early stages of dating a woman, you will have to compromise and accommodate her to a certain extent. But it's important to strike an early balance of give and take—both to maintain your attraction levels to her and to avoid setting any bad precedents for potential future relationships. So if you always feel like the "giver" or the "pursuer," there are simple ways to keep her doing an equal share of the compromising and accommodating.

Read on for a few clever ways to keep her on her toes—and give your toes a break for a change. Just like she has her sneaky little ways of keeping you in line, after reading the tips below, you'll have a few tricks up your sleeve as well.

▪ Break the "Rules" Every Once in a While

Instead of calling her on Wednesday to make plans for Saturday, try calling her that same morning for an impromptu date. And instead of waiting two days after that to call again, surprise her earlier . . . or wait a little longer. In other words, don't be too predictable with your phone calls; instead, mix things up. Avoiding dating "rules" will show her that you are in control and confident—and it will keep her guessing.

▪ Kiss Her Passionately, and Then Call It a Night

Would you like to keep her wanting more? Try this for a change: Plant a big, fiery kiss on her—and then call it a night. It will serve two purposes: First, it will keep you on her mind. And second, since you are the one to end the kiss and the evening, it will keep her wanting more.

▪ Don't Make Yourself Too Available

If she suggests getting together on Friday, suggest Saturday. If she wants Sunday, suggest Tuesday. Now, don't do this too consistently, or you may never land yourself a date. You just want to maintain the appearance of having a healthy social life. Hopefully, you actually have one, but for the sake of pursuing her, the illusion should be enough to keep her on her toes.

▪ Be the One to End the Phone Call

Why is this simple technique so successful? Mostly because the first few phone calls tend to determine the way a relationship will proceed. So after the conversation has run its course, politely end it and say good-bye. Using this trick just a couple of times will put you back in charge.

■ Let Her Do Some of the Legwork

If you are always the one calling and pursuing her, she probably has you on your toes most of the time. To reverse the roles, you need to let *her* do some of the work. Indicate this by your actions: At the end of the night, tell her to call you and stick to your guns. Yes, that means waiting for her to call. That way, she'll take some of the calling load and, more importantly, she'll take the position of the pursuer; this will give you back a degree of control.

■ Let Her Initiate Sex

Women almost always have the upper hand when it comes to sex—and she'll often use it to keep you on your toes. So switch things up for once and wait for her to initiate sex. If you're not seeking it out and bending over backwards pursuing it, then she'll have to be the one to pursue it. And that will *certainly* keep her on her toes.

■ Designate a Guys' Night Out

Instead of letting her dictate all your plans for the week, take the initiative to designate a guys' night out. This will let her know that you have other people in your social life. It will also keep her wondering what you're doing on your night out with the guys—some healthy jealousy never hurt anyone.

■ Keep the Upper Hand

Remember this important fact: Keeping her on her toes is not about acting like a jerk. Rather, it's about keeping a healthy and fun balance of control in a relationship. And after reading the above list, you should be in a good position to put yourself back in the driver's seat. So please drive with care.

5 WAYS TO KEEP THE UPPER HAND WITH WOMEN

1. No More Games

Every game a woman plays—playing hard-to-get, not returning phone calls, seeing how many hoops she can make a guy jump through—is a test in her mind. If you want to get the upper hand, you absolutely *have* to call her on her games.

2. Keep It in Your Pants

If you want the upper hand, you have to be the master of your domain—you can't let Little Elvis lead you around by the nose. So don't jump when she offers sex. Don't always be the one who initiates bedtime fun.

3. Develop a New Attitude

A lot of men act like a woman is doing them a favor by dating them, as if she's a great prize they have to prove themselves worthy of attaining. Turn this around—change your basic attitude. You're the prize, not her. It goes hand-in-hand with your essential confidence.

4. Have a Backup

At the start of a new relationship, the Upper Hand Guy always has a few strings to his bow, so before you get too involved, it's not a bad idea to have a backup woman in your stable if your new girlfriend goes ballistic. This way, it's easy to take a walk with the knowledge that you have somewhere to go.

5. Be Great in Bed

Unlike men, women can get laid nearly any time they desire, simply by asking. But women are far more discriminating about their sexual choices than men are—and they are looking for great sex. To maintain the upper hand, you have to make sure you're a champion between the sheets (for more on this, keep reading).

TOUCHING TIPS

When you are with women, breaking the touch barrier is important to show attraction, as well as to gauge how she feels about you. Within the first couple of meetings with a girl, it is necessary to break the touch barrier. Breaking the touch barrier doesn't mean crashing through it. Again, let the principle of "Leave Her Wanting More" steer your approach. Communicate your intents with brief, subtle touches.

It is important that when you do it, you avoid any sexual touching (i.e., avoid her breasts, butt, etc.), and your actions must be subtle so that she doesn't think anything of it. Here are six simple touching techniques:

■ *The Brush-Against*

When you are at the club, you can lightly lean against her so that both of your arms are touching each other. You can also brush against her as you are trying to get by her.

■ *The Small Back Wrap*

When you ask her out for a drink and she accepts, let her lead the way by placing your hand on the small of her back as she walks in front of you.

■ *The Legs & Feet Fly-by*

When the two of you are sitting down, let your leg lean on hers or your foot touch hers, leaving it there for a couple seconds too long before pulling away.

■ *The Teaching Touch*

Perhaps you are playing pool or miniature golf and want to show her how to hold the cue, putt the ball, or make the shot. Get behind her and do your thing.

6 PICKUP RULES WOMEN WANT MEN TO KNOW

Even as you're keeping your romantic target on her toes, playing the mystery man, you mustn't forget your intents—and nor should you let her forget them. Even as you maintain your elusiveness, you should take a certain directness in your approach, a confidence in pursuing your quarry. The six pickup rules that follow will increase your success rate with the women you're dating, the women you're pursuing, and allow you to project a self-assured, gentlemanly attitude in the process.

1. Don't Express Interest in Both Her and Her Friends

Hitting on more than one woman in the same social circle is a real deal-breaker. Not only will it make you seem like a player but shows you are forgetting one very important factor: In order to successfully pick up a woman, you have to make her feel special. And hitting on or expressing interest in her friends will certainly *not* make her feel special.

2. Make Her Feel Like She's the Hottest Woman in the World

Often, a woman will go for a man for only one reason: how he makes her feel. So if you make her feel like the most beautiful girl in the room, chances are she'll want to see you again. This will work in your favor in the long run too; if she's confident and comfortable with you, you'll reap the benefits in *all* aspects of the relationship.

3. Don't Avoid Complimenting Her If You Think She's Heard It All Before

In other words, don't avoid approaching her in the beginning and complimenting her later because you think you're not the first to do so. You might think that it's not worth your while to approach that beautiful girl standing in the corner. You probably assume that she's had umpteen guys chat her up before you. But consider this: most guys think that very same thing. Often, the prettiest girls get their share of catcalls on the street, but are seldom approached by nice, genuine guys. So don't be intimidated or assume she's heard it all before. Instead, if you keep it simple, she just may be grateful for some pleasant, sincere conversation.

4. Don't Use Pre-packaged Pickup Lines

Using a clichéd line will do one of two things: It will either make you look like you're trying too hard or it will make you seem inexperienced with women (which is even worse). Instead, keep it simple and just try to be sincere. You'll cut through the formalities and stand out from all the men who *do* use lines on women—and yes, there are many who still do.

5. Approach Her in Places Other than Bars and Nightclubs

In a bar or a nightclub, a woman is used to being approached by men, and she'll have her armor ready. What this means is that she may reject you simply because you approached her right after a man who annoyed her, or because you were last in a long line of men to talk to her. Furthermore, in nightclubs, as women are expecting to be picked up, they form a defensive shield against unwanted men. This will obviously work against you.

If you approach her in other places, though, you have the element of surprise to your advantage. In a supermarket or a coffee shop, for example, she won't be expecting to get picked up and might be pleasantly surprised by your gesture. Having said all that, do be mindful of approaching a woman who is shopping in sweatpants and appears in a rush—she probably won't be the most receptive subject.

6. Know When to Walk Away

Repeat this to yourself before you go in for a pick up: there's nothing worse than a clingy guy. Reading her body language is not only important to gauge when she's interested, but also to determine when to walk away.

For example, is she giving you eye contact or are her eyes wandering around the room? Does she look bored by the conversation? If you are giving her your best, most sincere maneuvers and she is still not responding, then cut your losses and move on.

And what if she is giving you all the good signs? You still shouldn't overstay your welcome. If you leave the conversation on a high note, you'll only leave her wanting more.

MAKE HER CRAZY FOR YOU

Human nature is very strange. People believe that if something comes at a low cost, it probably has little value, while if things are more difficult to possess, they are automatically of better quality and more valuable. This is where the expression "you get what you pay for" comes from.

The same principle applies to the dating game. In general, a woman will always cherish a friendship, but she will always go crazy for that charming man whom she had to work hard to get.

Give Yourself Extra Value

A man should never let himself be taken for granted. This usually happens when a person is perceived as having lower value. In general, you should take the necessary steps and eliminate anyone who is not willing to pay the price required to deserve you from your life.

One way to strengthen a woman's perception of you as a valuable companion is to limit your availability to her. Scarce and rare products are typically perceived as valuable ones; people are prone to place more value on elusive objects. By applying this same logic to yourself as an object of her interest and presenting yourself as a rare commodity, you will heighten your own value in her eyes. By not always being around her, you will be perceived as scarce and hence more valuable.

Scarce products are perceived as more valuable (e.g., gold, diamonds, rare baseball cards). People place more value on things that require more work and effort to achieve. If you are "rare" or becoming more "scarce," people will view you as more valuable. By not always being around your girlfriend (or prospective girlfriend), you will be perceived as scarce and hence more valuable.

WAYS TO INCREASE YOUR VALUE:

■ Do not always spend your time around her. In fact, you should be willing to withdraw your time and attention from her from time to time. Once in a while, cancel dates and don't always return her phone calls.

■ If a woman does something that angers you, do not be intimidated; let her know that you are angry (without losing your head). Men that do not stand up for themselves lower their value because women perceive them as free rides.

■ Let women know that you have morals you strongly believe in. For example, let her know politely that women who try to play head games with you are kindly escorted out of your life without hesitation.

Break the Chain

A woman will only have true passion for a man when she thinks that she is capable of losing him. By showing a woman that you are not chained up or addicted to her, you are conveying that you are confident and will not let yourself be taken advantage of.

On the other hand, if you put up with her abuse, head games, and disrespect for you, she will never experience the stress of possibly losing you and the passion will slowly disappear.

Introduce the Competition

Introducing some competition into a woman's life will make her realize that you are worth more than she may think. It makes you more attractive in her eyes, causing her to believe that she will have to work hard to *get* you.

This can be accomplished by inviting other female friends to join you on your group excursions. You can also add fuel to the fire by having names and numbers of other women around your house, car, and even popping out of your wallet when paying for dinner or lunch. If this doesn't get a woman jealous, it will definitely keep her on her toes. If she asks you about all these women, simply say they're friends of yours.

The first rule that every man should know is that scarcity brings value. Economics taught us that supply and demand determine the price or value of an object. This means that you should never make yourself available to a woman at all times.

When a woman thinks that you are easily attainable, your value drops *big time*. Hence, it is your duty to make sure that you know how to *walk the walk*. Confidence works in two ways, so let her know that you like going for what you want, and will move away from what you don't. By following these simple guidelines, it's guaranteed that any woman will go absolutely crazy with her desire for you.

RULE 4: ADAPT TO YOUR ENVIRONMENT

Certain pickup strategies may be universally effective ones, but pickup situations unfortunately aren't. You could meet the woman of your dreams just about anywhere. She could be at the gym, on a business trip, at the grocery store . . . even at the dog park.

As always, being prepared is key. You need the appropriate line of approach for the place and circumstances you're in, so you don't come off as insincere. In this chapter, you'll find tips for taking advantage of many different situations and environments you might find yourself in. But no matter where you are, remember to read her cues, and you'll be well on your way to a successful pickup.

APPROACHING WOMEN . . . ANYWHERE

Have you ever wanted to approach a beautiful woman, whether she just walked by on the street, or was sitting at an adjacent table in the same restaurant, but then simply sat back and rationalized that it was not the appropriate time to make a move?

---

9 COMMON MISTAKES

Unfortunately, some men don't realize that certain factors will deter a woman from accepting an advance or invitation from a total stranger. Here are the 9 most common mistakes men make when approaching a woman.

1. Forgetting a woman's safety & comfort zone: Most women will be on their guard when you first approach them. Accept her natural wariness and don't provoke it further by asking excessively personal questions or breaking the touch barrier too early.

2. Trying to fool women: Many men think that they can fool a woman into giving them their number. Women know when you're trying to pick them up, so don't beat around the bush. Be direct and let them know exactly what you want.

3. Acting like a pervert: Many men sabotage their best chances by keeping their eyes aimed down at a woman's breasts. Instead, keep your eyes locked onto hers.

4. Using pickup lines: Canned pickup lines are never recommended—especially when it comes to meeting women outside. Throw her a couple

---

Most men refuse to approach women on the street because they have no idea how to go about it. Hey, if it's hard enough approaching women in clubs (where the environment invites social communication), imagine how much harder it is when it comes to the outside environment.

Meeting women on the fly is never easy—especially because women are suspicious about strangers. But you never know who you'll meet. That could be your soul mate walking by. Why not take a chance?

---

of negative hits to give yourself the opportunity to showcase your personality, then be yourself.

5. Not closing the deal: Sometimes, a man puts so much effort into the pitch that he forgets to close the deal. There's no point in approaching a woman if you're not going to muster enough courage to ask for her number.

6. Approaching all women: If you get a phone number from one woman, don't make a move on another beautiful woman. Control yourself; if the first woman sees you, you can bet your dog's tail that she'll screen her calls.

7. Burning bridges: Just because she didn't warm up to you, it doesn't mean you have to insult her. If you get rejected, just bow out gracefully.

8. Lying: Some men have no idea to say when they approach women, so they choose to lie. Give her credit; they're not stupid—and what happens when she finds out you lied?

9. Thinking it's a marriage proposal: You're not about to delve into a marriage proposal; your life does not depend on this one stranger's decision. Relax; it's a simple approach—all you're going to do is say "hi" and make a friend (or a lover) . . . not a wife.

The Reality Factor

Even the perfect approach will not guarantee a date. Sometimes you might run into women who are already spoken for, don't have the time to stop and talk, are having a bad day, or are just not interested. In any case, don't blame yourself and don't let your ego take a hit. This is normal and happens to many men. Getting rejected by a stranger is not that bad and is part of the game. The important thing is to remember is that it happens often, but hey, every dog has his day.

In general, there are three basic situations where you're going to run into women unexpectedly: the acquaintance encounter, the repetitive encounter, and the first encounter. Adapt the following strategies to suit your situation.

Acquaintance Encounter

This usually happens at parties or friends' houses. She's usually the pretty girl that every single man has his eye on.

The Strategy: Before any other man has the courage to do so, ask the person throwing the party or the pretty girl's acquaintance if she's single, and if so, to introduce you to her.

Repetitive Encounter

This situation usually occurs in places you frequent often such as a restaurant (during lunch), the gym, or even on your way to and from work. It's not uncommon to run into the same faces, and sometimes one face is a little cuter than the others—especially when she's returning the eye contact.

The Strategy: Don't be shy. Instead, be confident, approach her, and say, "Hi, I notice you every day, and I'm taking this as a sign to come and talk to you. Do you mind if I join you?"

First Encounter

This situation occurs when you run into a woman for the very first time. The most common situation is when she walks by you either in a mall or on the streets. This situation has a very low conversion rate: women don't warm up easily to strangers. So don't feel bad if you get rejected. The important thing is that you tried and have nothing to regret.

The Strategy: As she walks by you, look for eye contact. As soon as you get it, smile and say, "Hi." If she gives you no sign, then just keep walking because she's definitely not interested. If she smiles back, it's a sign to make your move.

Then once she passes you, walk back towards her and say, "Excuse me, I'll never forgive myself if I let you walk by without getting your name." If she gives you her name, it's a really good sign. Ask her where she's headed and make small talk. Then say, "Well Mary, I'd love for you to have my number and I'd love to have yours as well, so that we can have an opportunity to speak again."

Remember, nothing ventured, nothing gained. Get out there and approach women. With practice, you'll be meeting women everywhere you go with confidence and ease.

HANDLING COMPETITION

So you know how to play the games required to get women right where you want them—and often, where they want to be. But you've probably noticed that you're not alone out there. Other guys, are also on the prowl, especially for the hotties.

Ever found yourself in direct competition with another guy over the same woman? Did you know what to do to win her desire?

Assess the Pickup Situation

Based on the dynamics of such a pickup setting, there are a few things you can do. You can either treat the competition as a "tool" to further your pickup, or ignore him. In any case, never forget that a single woman is fair game for all.

If he doesn't follow by the rules (e.g., he cuts in while you're picking up the woman), then he becomes an enemy. Even so, make sure to always focus on the prize instead of trying to outdo the other guy, which can look immature.

While in a three-way conversation with another man and your target woman, keep the conversation focused on her by asking her questions and making interesting general conversation related to what she's saying, rather than droning on about yourself. Remember, people generally think the best conversationalists are actually the best listeners.

Whatever you do, don't cling. Don't hang around and try to show off or pay her too much attention.

Watch Your Competition

Don't get distracted by your competition, but be aware of his intentions and actions.

Get Some *Alone* Time

Take the woman somewhere private in the nightclub, so the other guy won't see you; you'll operate better. If things are going less well or you think she likes the other guy more, you may need to try to separate her from him with some excuse like "Will you excuse us for a minute?" Then turn to her and say, "There's something I wanted to show you."

Lead her elsewhere in the bar and say something like "I didn't really feel like sharing your company with that other guy, and what I wanted to show you is that we can entertain ourselves better—just the two of us. Selfish, yes, but I've got other redeeming features." Taking her aside like this is a bold move, which may impress her, and buy you more time with her, or backfire. But you've got nothing to lose.

Accept Her Decision

In the end, if she likes your company better than the other guy's, then you've succeeded in seducing her and she'll stay with you. In any case, the woman is the final judge; you have to respect her decision. If she's interested in the other guy rather than you, bow out gracefully, then move on to somebody else.

Without horns to lock or duels to call, the modern man only has attractive words and actions to prove his worth versus other men. It's actually in competition that your tactics may just prove most useful.

By focusing on the woman and your mission rather than getting distracted by her other options, you stand the best chance of coming out victorious.

8 TIPS FOR NIGHTCLUB PICKUPS

Most guys think that nightclubs are a great place for action, yet they don't seem to have much luck. Even though bars and nightclubs are ground zero for pickup artists, being successful at it is not always as easy as it seems. Here are some tips to make the most of a great evening activity.

1. Pick the Best Real Estate in the Nightclub

Remember the three fundamentals of business: Location, location, location. How many times have you seen hot women in a bar from afar, but were stuck at a table with your friends? You want to be mobile and ready to nonchalantly be near a woman who interests you. You want a spot with good visibility and high traffic, so as to be able to interact with more people than if you're holed up in a booth in the corner. In the pickup game, it's also good to have an excuse for being where you are—in line for drinks at the bar, or for the restroom—so as not to look like a stalker.

2. Befriend the Bartender/Barmaid

Being connected, especially at a hot club, makes you look like a big shot, which can only help your chances. And who knows, you may just wind up picking up the barmaid.

3. Forget the Canned Icebreakers

Pickup lines are lame. Women consistently rank honesty and a sense of humor very highly as desirable qualities in a man. A pickup line seems too premeditated, which makes it seem dishonest, and to women dishonesty is threatening, not funny.

Humor is your fastest route in. Otherwise, ask her to help you and your friend resolve a debate—even if it means conjuring up a debate on the spot. Turn to your natural sense of spontaneity and playfulness when approaching women, and plenty of methods will occur to you.

4. Don't Go at It Alone

Two is a good number. Use a wingman. You can also use a wingwoman, which can really help, since having attractive female friends makes you look appealing to women. If your wingwoman is drop-dead gorgeous, it could be intimidating to women, but not if you explain she's a friend. The fact that you've got such a hot friend you can restrain yourself around (say something like, "I just know we work better as friends. I don't need to go there with her.") reflects well on you.

5. Meet All Her Friends

If she's with a group of friends, don't simply pick her up and ignore her friends. Introduce yourself to the group. As you will likely not talk to many of them very long, first impressions really count here. If you're with your buddies, introduce them to the women also. Let both groups mingle, rather than simply picking up one of the girls.

6. Dance Your Way In

If she's on the dance floor, put yourself in her line of sight. Get in her vicinity, then move into her dancing area naturally. At first, be sure to respect her personal space. Once you've gotten and held her eye contact for a bit, extend a hand to her as an offer to dance with you.

Don't use the closeness as an excuse to grope or start a full-on conversation. Hold your cards closer to your chest and save the intimate touching for later, once you've closed the deal. Then it's not groping; it's foreplay.

7. Don't Cut Another Man's Grass

If a woman is there with a man, and she seems to be flirting with you, let her make the first step to you. Don't move in while he's gone to the bathroom, for example, as this can create very awkward situations.

If a guy's got a flirtatious girlfriend, let him work it out with her, not with your jaw. There are plenty of fish in the sea.

8. Quit While You're Ahead

This is key. Unless it's obviously going somewhere right then and there, once you get her number, don't overstay your welcome. Leave the situation while you're ahead. Say good-bye and mention you'll call her to set up a date. At that point, ideally you would leave the club (you can make any excuse)—on a high note.

WANT TO PICK UP A BARMAID?

It's no surprise that most men would love to date or sleep with the local hot barmaid. One could even say that most men have, at some point in their lives, attempted to seduce a barmaid. And chances are, their success rate isn't too high. Why? Picking up a barmaid in her working environment and picking up a woman during her leisure time are two completely different things, and require two different approaches. Unfortunately, most men use the same generic pickup strategy on barmaids as they do on the female clientele.

Admittedly, there is no guaranteed technique that will make the barmaid fall head over heels, but these methods will at least prevent you from being shot down quickly.

The Right Approach

1. Smile and make sure to look straight into her eyes and ask her name before ordering a drink for the first time. Don't leave her a big tip; leave her a regular tip. Then make your exit, to dance, chat with your friends, or otherwise.

2. Now that you know her name, always use it and smile whenever ordering drinks. Don't use words such like "sweetie," "cutie," "baby," or "hey."

3. In the beginning, never try to make conversation during her busy hours. You have to remember that she's very busy and needs to concentrate. The last thing she needs is a pest who makes her confuse the orders. Respect her zone.

Besides, how interesting can you be if you have to interrupt her every two minutes? Your best bet is to show up early before the bar gets busy. This will give you more time to develop a conversation.

4. Never volunteer your name. Let her ask for it. It shows some sort of intrigue in what you have to say.

5. No compliments. Everyone else has told her before. To a barmaid, flattery means nothing. She hears it every night and has become immune to it—especially from a stranger. Instead, give her a negative hit. Try saying something like, "Your lipstick is running," while smiling.

6. Become her friend. That's right; don't show too much interest in her. Instead, concentrate on being a friend. Keep her entertained whenever she's not too busy.

7. Have an interesting conversation; talk to her about something other than the bar scene. Ask her what she does in her leisure time. Ask if she has a day job or goes to school. The idea is to show authentic interest in her life, not her body.

8. Learn to recognize and dismiss false buying signals. A false buying signal presents itself as a sign of romantic interest, but is symptomatic of something else entirely—oftentimes an ulterior motive. For example, a waitress's flirtatious tone and mannerisms may seem to indicate her interest in a patron, but any regular bargoer knows that it actually represents her interest in getting a healthy tip from him.

9. Asking for her phone number will lead her to believe that you are like all the others trying to get into her pants. Never ask her for digits; it's a dead giveaway that you're trying to pick her up.

10. After developing a good friendship (usually takes a few weeks), ask her what she's doing after work (assuming she has no boyfriend). Then ask if she'd like to go for coffee, or if she's tired, ask if she'd like to hang out on a Sunday afternoon. If she says "no," at least you tried and won't have any regrets. If she says "yes," now is the right time to exchange phone numbers.

There you have it: a simple yet effective approach. But before you make a move, make sure that she's actually interested in you, and not what you might tip her. You can avoid this by being aware of most barmaids' secret intentions and how they work. The best way for a barmaid to achieve her objective is to use her body language, beauty, and sexual appeal to convince men to be a little nicer—and open their wallets.

So what are the signs that would normally be good buying signals, but don't mean jack when you're trying to pickup a barmaid?

She Remembers Your Name

Of course she does; it's George Washington, and you're the guy who keeps tipping her with the juicy greenbacks.

She Offers You a Free Drink

Most barmaids are allowed to give away a certain amount of drinks per night to good paying customers. If you're a big spender, then don't give it much value, you've more than made up for it in repeat purchases.

She Smiles at, Waves, Touches, or Even Kisses You

It's called flirting for a dollar. The better she makes you feel, the more likely you'll tip her better. Some men actually believe that a woman would sleep with them because they give a $10 tip instead of a $5 one. The only thing this will get you is prompter service.

Now, let's look at some bartender-specific buying signals that can be taken as good ones.

Only Has Eyes for You

She makes the other customers wait while she listens to your conversation. It's a bonus if she always stays on the same side of the bar that you're sitting in.

Takes Away the Sexy Aspect of Her Job

She does not try to seduce her way into your wallet and complains about how hard it is to serve drooling, drunken men who are only interested in her body—not you, right?

▪ Personalizes Her Conversation

She enjoys talking about more important things in life than sex, booze, cars, and money. With you, she enjoys sharing her personal life.

▪ Asks Where You Hang Out

She's curious to know what you enjoy doing with your free time.

▪ Asks If You Have a Girlfriend

This one's simple: she's surveying the field and wants to know if you're available.

▪ Tells You What She Wants to Do With Her Life

She has ambitions and is letting you know that she doesn't plan to spend her whole life serving alcohol to a bunch of drunken men.

All these hints should give you a better indication of her authentic interest level in you.

DO NOT

- Buy her one of those roses that opportunistic jerks try to sell at bars.

- Keep buying her shots all night. She's probably not allowed to drink on the job and will just be pouring herself water and pocketing the money (or thinking you are the kind of guy that preys on drunken girls).

- Ask her for complex drinks just to appear suave. She's busy and she's heard it all before.

DO

- Work up the nerve to seal the deal, preferably before last call (only the real hardcores close the bar down, and she probably hates those guys). Tell her you're leaving, but ask her what she does during the day. Suggest you meet for coffee or a walk, but make sure you get her phone number.

Don't Be Jealous

Dating a barmaid is not without its hazards—especially if you're the jealous type. Remember that the same way you hit on her, another ten men will do the same each night she's working. Can you handle that?

Remember that if she wants to earn a nice paycheck, she's going to have to flirt and dress sexy for other men. Can you handle that?

Remember that you have to be on your toes 24/7 in order to keep her satisfied because there will always be a suitor waiting for you to screw up and take your place. Can you handle that?

If you answered "no" to any of these questions, then you might want to think twice before jumping into a committed relationship with a barmaid. Otherwise, enjoy the sex on the beach.

HOW TO PICK UP AT THE GYM

Believe it or not, the gym is probably one of the easiest places to meet women. It's not that hard for the average man to successfully approach his woman of choice at his favorite workout spot.

Be realistic; don't expect a miraculous overnight pickup strategy. You have to be patient and follow a few preparatory steps before actually approaching women. Once you've prepared yourself, you can move onto the task at hand.

The important thing to keep in mind is the main reason people attend the gym in the first place. If you believe that you are at the gym solely to pick up women, then achieving your goals will become slightly more stressful.

Instead, if you remain focused and remind yourself that your primary reason for going to the gym is to work out and get in shape, then you will have no problem bench-pressing some booty.

Here are five objectives to aim for. If you can achieve them, you'll definitely be the MVP of your health club, and women will be honored to make your acquaintance.

1. **Become friends with the owners and staff.** You can do this by simply saying, "Hi," and making small talk every single day.

2. **Learn the proper techniques of exercising.** This is important for two reasons. First, to make sure that your muscles are getting a proper workout, and second, you will need to know them later on, if you want to help a struggling woman with her exercises.

3. **Get in shape.** The competition is ferocious and the gym is full of big, knuckle-headed rivals. Women don't necessarily like big ape-like men, but they do appreciate a fellow who keeps in shape.

4. **Socialize with everyone—including men.** This is important because you will quickly become popular, and everyone will see you as the friendly guy. So when you approach women, they'll assume that you're just being friendly, like you are with everyone else.

5. **Speak to all women.** This includes fat, small, large, beautiful, and average looking women. Women are naturally jealous and very competitive, and when they see a popular man talking to all the women, they too want to be part of that clique.

When a hot new girl comes into the gym, everyone sizes her up. A few guys will go up to her immediately. Instead, lay back, get to know her first, and just say, "Hello."

Use the other guys to your advantage. Observe their mistakes and what to avoid before finally approaching her. In other words, establish an ongoing, non-threatening rapport, and then wait for clear "ask me out" signals.

GYM PICKUP DOS & DON'TS

Some men are oblivious as to how to behave in health clubs. Here are some tips to help you achieve your five main objectives a lot faster.

TURN-ONS

■ Smile, say, "Hi," and leave her alone for the rest of the work out—unless she invites you to stick around.

■ When you notice a woman struggling with her weights, spot her, but don't use this as an excuse to socialize with her—unless she invites you to stick around.

■ Gently point out when she's doing an exercise the wrong way, and afterwards leave her alone—unless she invites you to stick around.

■ Ask for a spot, but don't use this as an excuse to get her phone number—unless, of course, she gives it to you.

■ Be funny and charming: if you see that her water bottle is empty (after you make sure she has no earphones), offer to fill it up for her. Or if she has no bottle, bring her a glass of water and say, "You look thirsty." Don't be too serious; simply use this as an icebreaker to start a conversation.

TURN-OFFS

■ Stare at women and follow them around throughout their entire workout and you'll be arrested for stalking.

■ Don't flex in front of the mirrors—you'll look like a prima donna—and don't grunt or make loud, macho noises. You will sound like you're either having a self-induced orgasm or experiencing Chinese torture. Keep the grunting to a minimum.

■ Women hate men who are not hygienic. If you sweat too much, smell or never wipe the equipment, don't even bother to approach a woman. Your most important ally is deodorant.

■ It's okay to smell fresh and clean. But avoid drenching yourself in cologne and dressing like you're out at a dance club.

■ Don't comment or give compliments on body parts, like "Nice legs," "Your butt is shaped like a half-moon," or "I can tell that you work out a lot by your beautiful figure."

■ Whistling or making any other kind of courting calls will end up making you look like a desperate dud with a speech impediment.

■ Never touch a woman's body in any way even while helping her with the weights—especially if she is still a stranger.

■ Mention of anything that pertains to sex or including any sexual innuendo in your conversation will make a woman very uncomfortable.

■ Asking a woman if she has a boyfriend or husband, is like revealing your hand in a poker game. Be patient, and get to know her first; if she's unavailable, she'll let you know.

HOW TO SCORE A STEWARDESS

For most guys, these hostesses of the sky will never be more than mile-high club fantasy figures. With only a few hours to seal the deal, why even bother trying? Well, with the proper direction, a few hours is plenty of time. Play it smooth, follow this advice, and you might just get the ultimate upgrade into a whole new level of first class.

Sit in the Back of the Plane

Do everything you can to get a seat in the back, near where the cabin crew hangs out. You'll have a better chance of catching her when she is out of stewardess mode and you'll get to see what she's really like (and if this is even worth it). Keep your ears open for boyfriend talk or any other deal-breaking topics. There's no sense putting your dignity on the line if she keeps mentioning how much she misses her Mikey or lets something slip about her incurable rash.

Find Out Her Itinerary

You have to do a little intelligence gathering as quickly as possible in order to establish whether or not you should bother. As a bonus, finding out the particulars of her trip is also a wonderful icebreaker. If she's headed for a two-hour stopover before boarding another flight, don't bother; you won't have enough time to reap the rewards of your efforts. Ditto if she's on her way home: She'll be headed back to her own life, and "getting in" in this case will probably only be possible as a precursor to something serious. That's great if that's what you're looking for, but it's a major red flag for guys trolling for a something a little more casual.

What you are really looking for is a stewardess who is stopping over for a couple of days in a foreign city. She'll most likely be looking for something to do, and if you're smart, you will be able to provide that something. The ideal situation involves her having that stopover in your hometown. You get to show off your city while showing her a good time, and hopefully she will repay you with more than an insincere "thank you."

Pick the Right Time to Chat

As she will be busy, you have to judge when it's best to strike up a conversation. Your strategy will change according to your flight's duration. On an overseas flight, you have more time to take, while on a quick commuter jaunt, you have to work rapidly.

Regardless of how long your flight is, the time before drink or meal service is a bit of a write-off, as she has a lot to do. You need to establish a rapport before they roll out those carts, and then leave her to do her duties. That means that you have a really short window of opportunity to make your move. Hey, if this were easy, every guy and his uncle would be walking around with a couple of stewardesses on each arm.

Talk About Things You Have in Common

When you do get a chance to chat with her, you have to find common ground fast. Places you've both been, places you want to go, funny experiences you've had while flying—these are all topics she will be able to relate to. Asking her about customer horror stories is an easy way to get her to let her guard down and give you a glimpse of the real person beneath the smiling, professional persona.

It is then time to crank up the charm (but not too high, or the mask might pop back on). If you don't sense any sparks during the initial conversation, you will have to run a near-flawless game in order to make it work. Don't panic; just back off a bit and wait for another opportunity to make your move.

DO

■ Dress comfortably, but more importantly, dress well. This goes for any time you fly, but especially when you are trying to pick up a stewardess. Wrinkles are inevitable when flying, so you might want to wear wrinkle-resistant pants and a sturdy-collared shirt.

■ Have a few drinks, but don't get rip-roaring drunk. Sure, she'll remember you; unfortunately, she'll just remember you as the raging boozehound who kept hitting on her.

■ Call her by her name. She'll be called "Stewardess" by just about everyone else on the flight (who isn't trying to score with her), so she'll notice and appreciate the effort.

■ Bring an impressive book or magazine to read. Let her see *The Economist* or *The Great Gatsby* in your hands. It's a fairly easy way to convey a message of sophistication.

■ Get to the point. Time is limited, so don't beat around the bush.

Stewardesses see thousands of faces a week and a big proportion of the males in that lot make some attempt to flirt. So catching the eye of a stewardess is a long shot, and catching it enough to reap some benefits might seem nearly impossible. Well, someone once said that manned flight was impossible, but now the skies are filled with airplanes; and those planes are filled with stewardesses just ripe for the picking, provided you play it cool and try some of these tips. With that, and a little luck, the sky's the limit.

PICK UP WOMEN ON BUSINESS TRIPS

While business travel can be wearing at times, you might as well make it memorable. Take advantage of all the opportunities and encounters a dif-

DON'T

■ Bother her incessantly just to keep her attention; this is an automatic disqualification. Constantly ringing your call button will only ensure that you are the last person to get your pretzels.

■ Stink. It might seem obvious, but many travelers have rancid breath and raging B.O. But not you, right? Fill your carry-on with mouthwash, deodorant, and sample-sized cologne.

■ Try to tip her. She isn't a barmaid, and it's a massive slap in the face.

■ Order weird drinks or make odd requests just to stand out. Even though you have a job to do (pick her up), she has a more legitimate one (being a stewardess). You'll have to work around her schedule. Remember: no one said this would be easy.

■ Make innuendoes about joining the mile-high club. She didn't think it was funny when the first drunk idiot made the same crack to her years ago, and she thinks it is even less funny now.

---

ferent setting allows you to explore. In time, you might not even consider them business trips at all.

Even if you don't know a single soul in the host city before you arrive, social skills and a thirst for local flavor will always keep you entertained. How do you find out where to go? Figuring out the best way to spend your limited time in a city is easy enough, once you've figured out whom and how to ask. It just takes confidence and, as with everything, practice.

Ask Local Employees

If you're visiting another branch of your company, see if the employees recommend a certain lounge, nightclub, restaurant, etc. Make sure they know you're looking for a hangout where a bachelor can meet women. If you're asking a woman, it should be someone you'd be happy to go there with. If you're asking a guy, you can be a little more direct, inquiring about "fashionable" or "trendy" places with lots of action.

If you're at a company social event (happy hour, convention), you shouldn't have any problem picking out like-minded employees waiting for the first opportunity to bolt to somewhere happening. Introduce yourself to them and join them in their escape.

Tip: If you've already been in contact with a female colleague in the city you're visiting, flirt with her before the business trip. If you're attracted to her once you get there, you've got a plum situation waiting for you, and if not, she'll still be happy to help you. Who knows, maybe she's got friends you'll like.

Ask the Concierge

Although he might recommend some touristy places, tell him you want to meet local women in trendy hangouts.

Ask a Waitress or a Barmaid

These people often like to go out, and if you reveal that you're in town on business, it somehow sounds impressive. You can even do this in the hotel's lounge or restaurant.

Ask a Store Clerk

Clothing stores are good for this because the sell is longer so you have more time to get to know her and guess if her tastes are compatible with yours (which you're simultaneously finding out by the clothes she suggests).

Go Out and Pick Up

Now that you've picked your location, get to work. If you're lucky, you might manage to make a parlay between the venue recommendation and actually meeting the *recommender* (and her friends—bonus!) there, an instant informal date. But if it doesn't turn out that way, there are still lots of ways to meet people while away on business.

Approach a Group of Women, or a Woman by Herself

Play the "I'm from out of town" card and be straightforward, but not straight-laced. Phrase your introduction in a way that says you're a world traveler from out of town, and that you're curious to find out about some things. Remember: subtle innuendo is your friend.

Be Friendly with Guys as Well as Women

Striking up a conversation with another guy in the nightclub will provide you with a sidekick, even if he doesn't realize it. You can tell women things like, "My friend here says that local women are very easygoing. Is that true?" If you're getting somewhere, and especially if he's getting good vibes from the ladies, he'll be happy to let you put words in his mouth.

Remember that you're from out of town and alone. But rather than desperate and lonely, you're a suave, intriguing guy looking to provide local women with a tempting opportunity. Think it and you'll be it.

7 SUMMER PICKUP SPOTS

Summertime, in bigger and smaller cities alike, is marked by the plethora of flesh on view. People are feeling looser and more relaxed, and not in such a rush to get from one indoor venue to another. To you, that translates into more opportunities to meet women.

In summer, pickup settings abound, and we'll get to some of those in a minute. In the meantime, remember that women's confidence will be much higher, as they get hit on more when wearing sexier clothes—at least, the sexy women do.

Dressing lighter and sexier often marks more than a change of season. It's only natural for people to mirror the changing climate outside with a new-leaf emotional outlook. Knowing summer is an easier time for them to attract men, many women are more willing to come out of mediocre relationships and get back out there. They're looking to try new things—this is your chance to provide them with just that.

Anywhere you're encountering friendly women is a fair place to pick up. Things can happen anytime at or between venues with high meeting potential. Here are eight summer favorites, along with tips to maximize your success rate.

1. Official Opening Events

There's nothing like spending a summer evening on the patio at a brand-new bar. What's more, openings show that people are open to trying new things in search of a good time. You're likely to meet new people who are out to have fun, just like you. Just sit out on the terrace and pick your prey.

How to use this setting to your advantage: An opening is a social setting ideal for networking and mingling. But, as the place doesn't have an established vibe or reputation yet, women won't necessarily expect to be picked up, making it easier for you to talk to them, as they're not on the defensive. You can use the menu, the décor, or anything else about the new venue as a natural conversation starter.

2. Beach

Men love to look at women, especially when they're wearing bikinis. But looking, especially too much looking (that is, leering), won't get you anywhere. Approach the babes. Take part in some physical activities like volleyball or Frisbee, and invite women to play.

How to use this setting to your advantage: Ask a woman to join you to complete a volleyball team and get a game going, or ask to join a team yourself.

3. Company Outings

Big corporations organize summer gatherings like picnics, happy hours, cocktails, and so on. Attend as many as you can and hook up with female colleagues from other departments, or from your industry if you're mingling during happy hour with other corporations. But you have to play it even smarter than usual. A wrong turn could damage your reputation with colleagues. The closer to you your prey works, of course, the more careful you have to be.

How to use this setting to your advantage: This setting is open to mingling, and people will be friendly with each other. You won't be a complete stranger, even if you don't know a certain woman from your company. As at a house party, the fact that you're both there already gives you something in common which, if you don't have something funny to say, can serve as a conversation starter.

4. Park

Any high-traffic area like this is bound to attract women, who seem to enjoy people-watching as an end-in-itself pastime more than men do. Plus, women who choose to spend time in a park probably have a better idea of how to relax—an important characteristic in a potential partner for a casual, fun encounter.

How to use this setting to your advantage: Obviously there's no shortage of things to do in a park. But certain activities lend themselves well to mixing with strangers:

■ Get yourself a cute dog and walk him. A playfully nosy dog can do a great job of "inadvertently" introducing you to all sorts of people.

■ A Frisbee can be a great, wordless way to lasso a woman's attention. Simply catch her eye as she walks by and toss it gently her way—a spontaneous icebreaker with a built-in sense of fun.

5. Outdoor Concerts & Festivals

This is a great opportunity to talk to many women looking to dance, drink, and have fun. Learn the lyrics to a few of the performing band's songs and get out your lighter for the encore. Or even easier—and cheaper for you—are concerts of smaller-named bands at free folk and jazz festivals, a good place to find women with eclectic and inexpensive tastes.

How to use this setting to your advantage: You don't have to talk that much, and if the music is loud and/or good, you'd be stupid to. Simply be gallant by bringing her a drink or a bottle of water so that she doesn't have to walk all the way to the stand. Bear in mind that if she's with a bunch of girls (no guys), it might be a sign that she's single, along with her friends.

6. Camping

Get a few friends together and hook up with women on the campsite. They'll be easy enough to approach because you obviously share an interest: camping. Start a bonfire and sing some tunes on the guitar, take moonlit hikes to the lake or beach to gaze at the stars (chicks dig that), retire to your own tent, or just hang out in the woods. Romance and adventure are built right into such situations.

How to use this setting to your advantage: Be equipped and bring gourmet-but-still-roughing-it foods that are easily shared, like smoked oysters or mushroom caps stuffed with Brie or pesto, for example. These, along with sensual foods like fresh fruit chocolate fondue, show your sense of planning, impressing her while putting you in charge. Likewise, have beer, wine, or sangria to share with the ladies around your site. It might get cold at night, giving you a reason to keep her warm and maybe even share a sleeping bag. And since you're in the wild, her animal instincts might just come out.

7. Tourist Traps

Women from out of town will be vacationing at these popular hangouts. Offer to show them around town, always with the option of a "break" at your apartment. Hostels are a good place to meet female tourists, or the more popular bar strips.

How to use this setting to your advantage: Build a rapport with them and show yourself to be a straightforward guy for a bit before suggesting you'll show them around, or else their natural traveler's suspicion might put the kybosh on the whole thing before you even get started. Plus, you definitely don't want to come across as a professional tourist guide, but instead as a regular guy who wants to spend more time with these exceptional ladies. Once you've shared a few laughs, you are their on-the-spot, free guide who knows not just the history of the town, but also the little hidden restaurant and nightclub gems where your connections with the bouncers and managers will get you all in without any problem.

FIND WOMEN FOR WINTER SEX

Just because it's colder out doesn't mean your libido is hibernating, right? Read on to find out how to prepare for the season ahead so that, like a squirrel, you can expend your nuts 'til springtime.

It's natural to feel less adventurous in winter. Many of us carry a few extra pounds of winter fat, show less skin, our extra clothing sometimes feels like a chastity belt, plus it's logistically more difficult: there's all that outerwear to consider, and you can't just hang around outside figuring out what to do.

So in fall, people still have that summer freedom in their blood and the sense of urgency to take advantage of what's left of the warm weather.

For all of these reasons, it makes sense to put a special push in fall to make sure you've got plenty of possibilities for winter. Contact seeds planted during spring and summer that have taken longer to germinate—because of phone tag, busy schedules, etc.—often come to fruition in fall. The trick is to harvest them and pick some prize specimens to last you through the winter.

Because you're looking to extend things a little longer than you would the rest of the year, you might want to look for a few of the following qualities for a winter partner:

■ **Is emotionally low maintenance:** Always an important point, but especially so if you're trying to extend a casual fling without upping the emotional ante.

■ **Likes to stay in:** Means she's less likely to find competition for you.

■ **Has a car:** This adds flexibility to your arrangements if you simply feel like inviting her over to your place.

■ **Lives close by:** More convenient, and won't give her a false sense of importance by your traveling far to see her.

■ **Has a similar schedule to yours:** For example, a 9-to-5 schedule versus an evening shift or student schedule. This translates into fewer compromises for you.

BE CLEAR ABOUT YOUR INTENTIONS

Remember, if you find a woman who fits enough of these criteria to be a good winter fling, don't promise her anything just to ensure you land her, nor to extend things. If you're not looking to be a boyfriend, make this clear early on.

Along those lines, don't forget to take advantage of your past successes and call up a few Wild Cards to rekindle some hot times without having to lay all the groundwork.

Sure, winter can be long—but not if you plan in advance. When the colder weather comes along, be a good boy scout and always be prepared.

RULE 5: SET THE SCENE

You made a great first impression, and now she's coming back to your place so you can work your magic. Which means another chance to make—or break—that first impression. Never underestimate the role your environment plays in a successful seduction. It's your call: will your cleanliness and choice of décor impress her, or will first sight of your grubby hovel make her want to flee?

THE ULTIMATE PLAYER'S PAD

We all know that if a woman you've just met agrees to come back to your pad, you're doing very well and the toughest part is behind you.

Aside from the way you carry yourself, there's no better way to set the mood than by having an inviting and impressive pad. Suave décor and a few key elements are all it takes to turn your conquest into an adventure for her and, as a result, for you.

It's one thing to have a stylish, trendy apartment; it's another to have one that you can't move around in. The key here is to be tasteful in your choice of décor, but remain functional, cozy, and comfortable. Having a trendy apartment should not substitute for comfort, or restrain you from wanting to lounge in your den after a long day's work. It shouldn't stop you from watching a great movie, for fear of dirtying your precious designer leather couch.

Your place should be your place; it shouldn't veer too far away from your style or your taste. Keep in mind that you are going to be spending more time in your place than anyone else.

Here are some essentials to have in your pad in order to impress the ladies. Many of the items listed here are not direct sexual aids so much as mood setters that will improve her comfort level and decrease her inhibitions.

Collections

Art

Beer posters or anything with fluorescent colors are out. Vintage posters are cool, but get all posters framed or mounted—stick tack and tape, or even finishing nails, are for students. Original art is always good, provided that it's nice, which can be hard to do on a budget. Be unique. If you're a good photographer, frame some of your work and hang it.

Books

Put books that you actually like (it will look too pretentious if you display books that you haven't even read) on nice shelves. Also, coffee table books on art, architecture, or travel are good conversation starters, and are easy to leaf through whenever she has to keep herself entertained while you're occupied for a few minutes.

Vintage Items

For example, collections of old cameras, old appliances, posters, or vinyl records add a certain feel, and give the impression you're a guy with interests.

How will this help you get laid? Not only do such cultural items, especially your own photos, provide a springboard to many great conversations, they also make you look like a guy (and you may even be such a guy) who takes the time to appreciate beautiful things and details rather than some beer-guzzling bedpost-notcher. On an unconscious level, a woman will take your interest in culture as an indication of good taste, and will feel complimented that said taste has chosen her. By showing her who you are in such a way, you've boosted her spirits without uttering a word. Plus, women like a nicely decorated home more than just a functional pad, and will feel more relaxed in one, which adds up to fewer inhibitions and a better romp.

Mood Setters

Nice stereo

Indicates you have good taste and put a priority on enjoyment. It will also enhance your enjoyment of the matter at hand. Wireless speakers are a nice, convenient touch.

Music collection

Always have some female-friendly music on hand. That doesn't mean you have to run out to pick up some explicitly feminine CDs; just opt for the music in your collection that females have previously expressed an appreciation for. And no Finnish death metal.

Sensual lighting

Dimmer switches or colored lighting is always a plus. You can also use candles, as they tend to give the atmosphere an added allure. Avoid lava lamps, though, unless you're going for a kitsch collection look.

How will this help you get laid? These touches set the mood and comfort level at a much more unconscious level than art and books. Just try making a move on a woman with fluorescent lighting overhead and death metal on the stereo if you don't believe this.

Natural Props

Cute but manly dog

Getting a dog for pick-up purposes is a topic unto itself, but suffice it to say that if you're going to get one, you should get a friendly dog that is cute, but not too much so—you don't want women to think you're walking your girlfriend's dog. A poodle or Shih Tzu will send the wrong message. Try a pug, a Boston terrier, a Jack Russell terrier, or even a Lab.

Aquarium with exotic fish

Less cuddly than a dog, but pretty things please pretty girls.

Plants

Vegetation (no, not as an activity) really adds both an aesthetic and a homey touch. Even if you haven't much of a green thumb, have at least one in the corner in case she loves plants.

How will this help you get laid? All of these items demonstrate that you're able to take care of something, and thereby reassure her that you'll be attending to her needs shortly.

Extra Touches

Nice carpeting or hardwood floors

Industrial carpeting doesn't really set the right tone, nor does linoleum. Think of feet as the roots of our comfort, and try to nurture those roots.

Piano

Gives your pad a unique element of style. If you can't afford a piano, another instrument, like a guitar or saxophone, for example, will do the trick. It's best if you actually play the instrument, but you could always say it makes the place feel homey, and that you plan to learn it some day.

How will this help you get laid? As with all elements of style in general, these touches round out the whole picture, giving you a certain je ne sais quoi.

Bedroom

King-size bed

A must for good sex, and for good sleep afterward, a big bed is inviting as soon as it's seen.

Comfortable bed covers, sheets, and pillows

High-quality percale or even silk or satin sheets; women notice these things more than we do. Get some comfortable sheets, comfortable enough that she'll want to lie under the covers.

Massage oils

To get foreplay started on the right, um, hand. If you have just the right scent (jasmine, vanilla, etc.), she will give in to you easily—the trick is to avoid her sexualized parts in their entirety during the rubdown. Then ask her to reciprocate the favor.

Scented oils or incense

As mentioned, scents have a great effect on mood (think of fresh baked goods and the ensuing salivation), and the right smell can set an exotic mood. The effect of a smell is not proportionate to its volume, however; dousing yourself in cologne is more likely to repel women than attract them.

How will this help you get laid? Your bedroom should be as comfortable as possible, a veritable pleasure palace, and all of these elements will add to that. Again, comfort decreases inhibitions.

Food & Beverages

A well-stocked bar

Have chilled white wine and an assortment of female-friendly spirits on hand—vodka, gin, and, for the crazy gals, tequila. Cranberry, orange, and pineapple juice, as well as some tonic, should cover your mixing needs.

Chilled bottle of champagne

It might go over better if you already knew you were inviting her over (you bought it with her in mind), but you can always say you just happen to have it in the house.

Fresh strawberries

Go well with champagne, and are also quite sensual. Feed her, let her feed you, and then you can eat each other.

Chocolate

Have you ever met a woman who dislikes chocolate?

Espresso machine

Gives a luxurious feel to your home for those who like coffee, and can be used as a conversation starter, or simply to keep her awake for more sex.

How will this help you get laid? Any woman will expect you to have at least something to drink on hand, so you might as well make it something tasty and classy. Champagne makes any occasion feel more special, and also gives an excellent airy, sexual buzz. Chocolate and strawberries (or better yet, chocolate-dipped strawberries) are an excellent touch. Remember: a woman who feels a little pampered will be apt to return the favor . . . somehow.

Bathroom

Whirlpool bathtub

Cuddling in a tub makes for a good, relaxing time.

Hand-held showerhead

Set it to pulse and apply to her nether regions while you caress her body with your lips. She'll appreciate this big time.

Terrycloth bathrobe

She can wear yours. If you live alone, are supposedly single, but have two bathrobes, you'll start to look like, well, a player. Even if she can imagine that you get around, you don't want to throw it in her face. You can wear boxers or perhaps another, less nice robe that you can dismiss as your "old one."

How will this help you get sex? All these elements will take the edge off in the room where she's most likely to feel uncomfortable. A whirlpool is the kind of thing you can plan an evening around, with some candles, wine, and soft music. And the bathrobe has the added bonus of being easy on, easy off for repeat sex. Between rounds, she can feel dressed without having to actually get dressed.

Note: Don't keep any potentially embarrassing medication or ointment somewhere she might end up looking, like in the medicine cabinet.

In General

■ Get rid of clutter: A clean but stuffed place is not the effect you're going for.

■ Clean your pad: An empty, dirty place is just as bad as a clean, cluttered pad.

■ Keep it smelling good: Use air fresheners to give your pad a constant fresh scent. Potpourri, incense, or scented oils also do the trick, and plants will help.

■ Tissues: Keep tissue boxes around—makes things convenient for any little emergency. Keep nice, soft toilet paper in the bathroom—a small but important touch.

The overall message here is that surroundings directly influence mood. Unlike, say, clothes or sex toys, it might be hard to see the correlation between the money you spend on your pad and the quality of fun you have in it. But believe me, women are more attuned to these details than men.

So after making an effort to attract a woman, why not ensure that you can both enjoy the fruits of your pickup to the max with a comfortable environment that lets her feel less inhibited?

MAKE YOUR PAD SEX-FRIENDLY

Here are some additional details you might want to consider for those times a woman decides to spend the night.

Be Messy Within Reason

Contrary to popular belief, women don't want you to scrub your apartment spotless before they come over for the first time. They want it to be just the way it always is. If you make too much effort to clean up your pad, it looks, well, like you're trying too hard. This makes women nervous and generally uncomfortable. Hence, a little bit of "lived-in" clutter is acceptable.

Indeed, success despite a messy place is entirely possible too. But why add any more obstacles to your quest for sex? Your best bet is to maintain a state of general order and cleanliness around your homestead; just don't make it look like you scoured the place top to bottom with a toothbrush.

Clean Your Bathroom

Because most women are born with the neat freak gene, the bathroom has got to be kept reasonably clean. If your bathroom is too funky, they have one more reason not to spend the night. Keep at least two big, clean towels in the bathroom and designate one as "hand washing only."

Stock the bathroom with extra essentials like hand soap, a new unopened toothbrush, toothpaste, and mouthwash. Finally, put down a bathroom mat that she won't be afraid to step on.

Adjust the Room Temperature

Once you get her in your clutches, you don't want her to leave, so offering comfort in your surroundings is key. Women can be acutely sensitive to temperature, so prepare for them to be hot or cold when you are not. At 65 degrees, you might feel fine, while she has goose bumps. So always have an extra blanket handy.

On the flip side, women also hate to sweat. So it pays to invest in a powerful fan if you don't have access to air conditioning.

Keep Your Linen Clean

Women will notice your sheets and pillowcases, so make sure they are sharp-looking, and, more importantly, clean. Pleasant odors and images elicit pleasant reactions, so ensure that your sheets are stain-free and smell like fabric softener.

Set Up Some Entertainment

In your room, put together an entertainment system view of the bed. This way, once she's lying down, there's yet another reason for her to stay there longer. And showing a movie after sex might just buy you time to go for a second round.

Prepare Extra Clothes for Her

As a final word on comfort, it's always good to have an extra T-shirt and pair of boxers handy for her to sleep in, if the need arises.

Keep Your Pad Smelling Pleasant

First off, it's vital to keep your pad smelling good. Researchers have found strong evidence that estrogen makes women's noses more sensitive than ours. This means that whatever smells bad to you smells worse to her, so keep shoes and dirty laundry out of your bedroom. In their place, use a citrus plug-in air freshener or light some scented candles.

Taking a girl to your place is always going to give you the advantage when you make your move. So ensure that once she passes through your doorway, she's stimulated in every room, not just in your bed.

RULE 6: FOREPLAY FIRST

Maybe your newfound techniques have secured you a parade of casual lovers circulating through your bedroom. Maybe you've gone a step further and landed yourself a girlfriend—perhaps even a prospective wife. Whatever the case may be, you've moved from the bar to the bedroom, and you're going to need a new set of skills to accompany that transition. It's time to mold yourself into a great lover, a process that begins with mastering foreplay.

THE IMPORTANCE OF FOREPLAY

There was a time in which "foreplay" was considered something that a man had to do to get his partner ready for sexual intercourse. Today, foreplay has become an integral part of the whole lovemaking experience. It is true that impromptu sexual encounters without foreplay can sometimes be some of the best sexual experiences, but in general, most women will agree that good sexual encounters should include long and sensual foreplay. A more vigilant form of foreplay will bring increased pleasures to both partners, and make the lovemaking experience more enjoyable.

Most sex experts agree that there is no such thing as spending too much time on foreplay. The trick is to start intercourse when both partners are peaking with excitement and having a hard time controlling their desires.

What Is Foreplay?

What is foreplay? Foreplay can encompass a wide range of activities, including undressing, kissing, petting, and oral sex. Why is foreplay so important? First of all, men who cuddle and kiss their partners and know how to enjoy sensitive foreplay will often find that their partners will not only enjoy sexual intercourse more, but also reach orgasm more often. Most women need prolonged stimulation in order to reach a complete arousal, and foreplay will provide them with the required stimulation.

No Ultimate Foreplay

There is no such thing as the ultimate foreplay, and it's not about pressing the right buttons in the right order. It is about understanding what makes your partner tick and delivering those things that make her experience intensely pleasurable. There are many ways to give your partner extreme sensations, and it all begins with her brain. Simply tell her how beautiful she is and how much you appreciate her sensual body. By complimenting her appearance, especially if her confidence level is low, you give her added security and excitement, as well as more good reasons for her to go all out with the foreplay.

Set the Mood

Pay attention to romantic details. Creating the right environment for sexual intercourse is crucial, especially at mature stages in the relationship. Make sure the room is warm, the lighting subdued, and the sheets clean. Once the mood is right, take the time to undress her—the very act of removing your partner's clothes can be an important part of successful foreplay. Many have found that undressing increases eroticism, and that it can stimulate and intensify the feeling.

Kissing and Foreplay

Go slow; begin by kissing and caressing her. A kiss is usually the first physical expression of love and desire, but it is also often forgotten during sexual intercourse. During foreplay, one should kiss every part of his partner's body and not be restricted to the mouth. Most women complain that their partners don't kiss long enough and rush the movement directly to the genital area. Don't be shy to experiment on every part of her body and remember to prolong the foreplay with more kissing and caressing.

Learn During Foreplay

Use foreplay as a learning experience. Foreplay is the perfect time to figure out what your partner likes, and without a little exploration you will never understand what she really needs to be fully stimulated. Don't be shy; ask for feedback, and give her your own. Both partners benefit from good communication during foreplay and lovemaking. Also, without cutting the intensity of the moment, ask her what she really likes and what makes her go wild.

As a general rule, if she is satisfied with her sexual experience, she will usually make sure that you are satisfied as well.

THE POWER OF ANTICIPATION

Teasing and anticipation are a big part of sex. How many times has the build-up to sex with your woman been as good, if not better, than the sex itself? That said, it's time to master the skill of making her want it and not giving in to her right away, in order for her (and you) to enjoy sex more than ever.

During the Day

In the morning, tell her that you have something exciting planned for that evening, but don't tell her what it is. Let her mind work on it. Even though it seems predictable if you tell her that you plan to seduce her that night, it builds anticipation as she spends the rest of the day thinking about what's going to take place that evening.

When She Gets Home

When she gets home after work, quietly lead her to the washroom, where you will give her a warm bath. Glide a washcloth over her body and make sure to cover every inch of her. Then, give her some alone time so that she can rinse off and dry herself.

Once out of the washroom, welcome her into the bedroom and lay her down on the bed. Set the mood with some sensual music and a nice, long massage.

If you've done this effectively, she should be quite comfortable—and sexually aroused.

Before You Kiss Her . . .

Tease each part of her body. Kiss around her lips, give her a peck, and move around her mouth. Exhale onto her neck before you go in for a deep kiss. Move your lips lightly around her cheeks and under her chin.

Then, after kissing her aggressively, pull back and leave her wanting more.

Before You Play With Her Breasts . . .

Touch around her breasts and contour them with your palms. Slide your fingers between them lightly. Touch her nipples with the middle of your palm. Brush against her breasts with your lips.

Before You Perform Oral Sex . . .

Kiss and lick around her vagina and caress her inner thighs. And just like that, cut her off. She'll go crazy, but when you start again, she'll be much more turned on and closer to orgasm.

Before You Penetrate Her . . .

Enter her vagina for just a second with your fingers or your tongue. Penetrate her with only about an inch of your penis, just for a short moment. It may take some serious discipline on your part, but if you can manage it, she'll be in a near frenzy.

Suck on Her Fingers and Toes

Digits are very sensitive to touch. This is a unique feeling most women enjoy. Carefully put one of her fingers into your mouth, suck on it a little bit, then move on to the next one.

Note: not all women are comfortable with having their toes sucked.

Play With Her Hair

Move your hands through her hair, tugging on it gently. Slide it across her face and her lips.

Kiss that Hip Spot

Run your index finger around that little spot where her hipbone meets her belly. Then, give that spot a little kiss on both sides.

Hinder One of Her Senses

Blindfold her or tie her hands to the bedpost. Leave her with no idea as to what's going to happen next. Then, stimulate her by running a variety of objects over her body or using your mouth in strategic spots.

Building anticipation is no easy feat for most guys, as we tend to get excited as well. But with time and practice, you can learn to tease her, maintain your self-control, and be the best she's ever had.

---

4 FOREPLAY TIPS

Here are four tips that will help you turn everyday foreplay into something that will have any woman you seduce begging you to put it inside.

1. Talk & Tease

The power of suggestion can be as great as the sex itself for many women. If you can describe how you want to touch her, where, and with which of your body parts, she'll visualize it easily and eagerly.

2. Get Started in Public

If your girlfriend doesn't cringe at the thought of public displays of affection, try doing some fun things in public. Fun things like patting her ass in a restaurant, kissing her passionately while having drinks at a bar, or dirty dancing at a nightclub.

---

6 FOREPLAY MOVES SHE HATES

Since women are such an overly polite bunch, they often ignore the small—yet slightly irritating—things you do during foreplay. Really, she stays quiet to save face, and though you might think it's your embarrassment she is saving, it is really her own. She might be a little timid when it comes to telling you what moves she prefers, so she just shuts up and puts up.

The following are suggestions to help you avoid the things you might be doing wrong during foreplay. No matter how skilled you think you may be in these areas, read through each foreplay blunder to make sure you've got your moves down pat.

3. Strip Down

No need to dance for her while you take off your socks, but do remove your clothes slowly (especially if you're fit). Start by removing your socks, then your shirt, then your pants, and then your underwear.

4. Watch Some Sex & Kiss Her

Porn is a great way to get you and your girl in the mood. Put on something that both of you can enjoy (preferably other couples having sex), and lay naked with each other while you watch it.

Every now and then, stop watching the movie and kiss her, or play with her body. Make sure to pay more attention to her than you do to the movie.

And there you have it. Four easy ways to drive your girl crazy. Of course, you don't have to do them all in one day. Make foreplay an anytime, anyplace part of your life. Keep things lively, fun, and erotic, and she'll keep coming back for more.

1. Being Too Rough

Men generally prefer a firmer, more aggressive touch, so in turn they touch women how they themselves would like to be touched. Unfortunately, this doesn't really work because, generally, women like to be touched softly—"caressed" is a good word to describe it. So, next time you are doing anything to your girl and you are in doubt as to whether she is getting off, try doing it a bit softer and see how she responds.

The rule: If in doubt, ease up. It is far easier for her to ask you to go harder than to ask you to be gentle. Start with a very gentle touch and then build up the level of intensity. This works extremely well when performing oral sex, and allows you to learn without her explicitly instructing you; her responses will tell you if you are going the right way or not.

2. Using Repetitive Moves

When someone rubs the same spot for a long time, it gets irritating. Women are often assaulted with the kind of man who, after being told that something is "really good," decides to keep on doing it . . . over and over again. He also continues to use this move during every foreplay session, which can make things stagnant and boring after a while.

The rule: Changing activity or positions regularly is far better than running the risk of overdosing her (and you!) with repetitive touching. Repetition only serves to desensitize her and, eventually, bore her to tears. Keep it interesting—and keep her sensitive—by changing where you touch her. For example, start kissing her mouth and then move down her body— neck, breasts, arms (inner elbows, inner forearm, and fingers), stomach, inner thighs, and vagina. Instead of ending at her vagina, head down to her toes or back up to her breasts and neck.

3. Falling Back on Routine

Being boring in bed is normally the result of a distinct lack of imagination and, of course, a lack of "training." As opposed to being too shy and doing what we think is right (perhaps being too firm or being repetitive), training gives us the confidence to try new things.

The rule: It's all about trial and error. Try different strokes and different pressures and then ask her what it feels like. Don't forget, she will also be in "training" mode, discovering what she likes and doesn't like. Never assume that just because she hasn't complained, you are doing a good job. She just might not want to burst your bubble by telling you that you aren't the sex god you thought you were. Don't assume you know everything and she won't be afraid to tell you how to do something. Be a good student and the rewards shall be yours.

4. Being Aggressive During Oral Sex

Some of you will have partners who just don't like oral sex. There can be a number of reasons for this, but the biggest one of all is that you probably just don't do it right. One major causes of "not doing it right" is having a dry mouth when you start. Another is being too hard or even biting. Lastly, there's also the common problem of heading for her sweet spots far too quickly.

The rule: Keep a drink handy if you intend to go down on her. A sweet drink is good because it kick-starts—and keeps—the saliva flowing. Sugar-coated saliva is smooth and allows for gliding. Water will do, but it isn't ideal.

Start off with the lightest touch possible, and keep doing this until she starts to wriggle and push against you. When she starts to push against you, don't just go for your life—back away from her so the pressure remains the same as when you started (the opposite of what she wants). This will drive her crazy (in a good way, but don't go too long like this or she might smack you), and then you can start to slightly increase the pressure. A warm, relaxed, slippery tongue is divine when applied correctly—you know this.

On a sharper note, it is important to never bite her vagina, ever—it hurts. Gentle biting on other parts of her body may be erotic (for example her back or buttocks), but sensitive areas are just that—sensitive. Nipples and vaginas are pretty much "no-bite zones" unless otherwise requested. Biting *can* be extremely sexy when done properly. "Properly" means without drawing blood, leaving a mark, and/or hurting her. Unless she asks you to bite her hard, go easy with the fangs.

Men are always accused of "heading for the sweet spots" right away instead of taking the necessary time to turn a woman on properly. This, unfortunately, is not without truth. Some of you make a bad habit of heading south after a couple of nipple twists, a bite, and a spank. Women need far more stimulation and foreplay than you do, and if you don't respect this biological fact, you may find yourself desperate and dateless. Take your time and learn to read your woman.

5. Twisting Her Nipples

Nipple twisting is what sexually uneducated men do, and it is a dead giveaway that you don't actually know what you're doing. The truth is, nipple twisting is not erotic or sexy, and it doesn't feel good—it hurts. Unless you are specifically asked to do this, don't. If she wants it hard, she will likely tell you.

The rule: When touching a woman's nipples, you may gently pull, suck, lick, run a finger or thumb over the top of them, rub them gently between your fingers or even gently touch them with your teeth (the trick to this is to touch the nipples with your teeth, then wiggle your bottom jaw from side to side slightly and slowly, so the teeth graze the nipple crossways). There are plenty of other things you can do with her nipples and breasts, so use your imagination.

6. Missing Her Clitoris

You may be trying really hard to work your magic down there, but sometimes it's easy to feel a little lost, causing you to miss the clitoris. Remember that she has four vaginal lips: two outer and two inner. It's not the easiest thing to work around especially because you don't exactly get to have a good look at it much of the time.

The rule: The easiest and most effective way of getting to know a vagina is to get busy with your mouth and your hands. Look at what you're doing while you feel it, so other times when you can't see it, you can do it simply by touch. The clitoris can be hard to find if it is not aroused, and some women's are deeper set than others. You need to figure this out, and you may have to ask her to point it out to you if you are unsure. Yes, she would love it if you "just knew," but if you don't, learn. When the clitoris is aroused, it will stick out like a little hard bud under the skin. If you touch her gently, you should be able to feel it.

In regards to the deceptive little labia majora and minora, go right down to her perineum (the patch of skin between her anus and her vagina) and work your way back up. Make sure to always have slippery moist fingers when handling her vagina—even if she isn't wet just yet, it gives her the impression she is, which is a turn on.

Mastering Her Domain

With a bit of practice, the role of the klutzy amateur in bed can be left firmly in the past, where it belongs. We've all made hideous and painful mistakes during foreplay by biting, slobbering, repeating ourselves, and being boring. Women's bodies need different sorts of stimulation to get them ravenously horny and morph them into the raging sex goddesses you know they are capable of becoming.

The best advice that can be given to a man is to practice his craft. Being a pliable and willing student will take you far. The fact that you aren't so stuck up to admit you don't know everything (including, but not limited to, knowing where your girlfriend's clitoris is) makes you cute and somewhat vulnerable and makes her like you all the more. Ego gets in the way of good sex more than any other single thing, so don't let your sex life suffer for it.

9 WAYS TO TEASE YOUR WOMAN

Women love it when a guy is able to maintain sexual control and bring her to a whole new level of sexual experience. In order to perform this task, however, you have to have a great amount of self-control.

If your mindset is to drive her mad with passion, then that's what you will end up doing. You don't need an accent (although speaking a Latin language would help), and you don't need a bunch of props (well, maybe some). What you do need to get her motor running are a vivid imagination and the will to get your way.

Follow these nine tips to tease her to unknown heights.

1. Start Talking Dirty

What's the best way to turn a woman on? Via her brain, of course, and if you can learn to talk in a way that gets her mind venturing into a myriad of sexual fantasies, then you'll have her itching to get on top in no time.

Tell her what you're thinking. Give her a great visual about what's going to take place. Tell her how you plan to undress her slowly while caressing each body part as you unveil it slowly. Tell her about how you plan to use your tongue to arouse certain areas like her neck, back, and inner thighs.

Depending on how she communicates with you, pick up on her dialogue and follow suit using appropriate sexual language. Do you talk dirty to her in bed? Does she like it when you get nasty, or does she prefer a more romantic approach?

Use your knowledge to seduce her over the telephone, before you head out the door, or even while you're sitting in the living room watching television together. Your objective is to make her envision all the dirty things you want to do to her and, above all, that you desire her fully.

2. Massage Her Body

The idea is to massage her body in places that men don't normally head for when they're in the mood for sex. You can use a massage to awaken all those sexual senses by actually avoiding all of her sexualized body parts. Hard to believe? Believe it.

Sit behind her and begin by massaging her temples lightly with your index and middle fingers on either side. Gradually make your way to the roots of her hair and use your fingertips to massage her head. This is where you take complete control and subtly pull her hair by the roots, bringing her cheek to yours. Ask her if she likes what you're doing. Yes? Then you'll up the ante.

Whether she's naked or in lingerie, have her lie on a bed and begin by massaging her back lightly. Make your way down her back and get close to her buttocks, but don't touch them; skip over the area and move down to her ankles.

Massage her ankles and make your way up her calves and then up to her slightly parted thighs. Knead them lightly and make sure to get between her legs and close to her vagina, so that her lips part, but don't touch it at any point.

Have her turn around and begin massaging her neck, her shoulders, and her arms. Then make your way to the sides of her body and outline her breasts, but don't touch them. Even massage her chest between, not touching, her breasts.

Make your way down to her tummy and hips. Open her legs so that her vagina is exposed to the air. Massage one thigh at a time, using your hands to rub each leg decisively. Go all the way to the top with your hands so that you're almost touching her outer lips, but don't. Not even if she asks you to. Right about now, either she'll jump you, or you can always continue the massage until she just about reaches orgasm.

3. Lick Her Clitoris

So it's not rocket science, but it is something that many a man doesn't know how to do. You need to tease her clitoris by touching it oh so gently with your tongue. Make sure the surrounding air is cool and not hot. Women have been known to say there's nothing quite like the feeling of cool air on a hot, moist vagina.

Spread her legs, and slowly make your way down to her sexy spot. Put your face near it and let her see you inhaling her aroma (hopefully, you like the scent and she's a fresh woman). Next, stick out your tongue and make the tip hard. As lightly as you can, let your tongue meet her clitoris, and then remove it.

Start doing this at a quicker pace, but all the while, continue to simply touch your tongue against it. If you'd like, you can begin to lick quickly, but the point here is to drive her crazy.

4. Look Hot for Her

If your woman is with you, it's because she thinks you're hot. So it's about time you began looking the part. Although this works best for guys who are fit, just about any guy can look great if he sets his mind to it.

Start dressing better and even undressing better. Rather than ripping off your clothes until all you're wearing are your boxers and socks, take off your socks first, unbutton your shirt and your pants, then remove your shirt, and finally remove your pants. Now give her a moment to admire you.

Women love to see a man come out of the shower with some water still on his body and a towel wrapped low around his hips, low enough that she can see a hint of pubic hair.

The bottom line is, if you feel good and look good, she'll think you're hot, so show her that you are.

5. Kiss Her, But Don't Touch

This one is quite difficult for most guys because they habitually use kissing as a means of getting into the nitty-gritty of lovemaking. But this time, you're going to torture her (and perhaps yourself) by sticking to the mouth area and nowhere else.

Many women complain that their men don't kiss them enough, so make the effort to slip her the tongue every now and then. Put your hands on either side of her face and bring her mouth to yours.

Spend about three full minutes kissing her mouth slowly and passionately. This will not only freak her out and turn her on like crazy, but it'll leave her with a lasting impression, especially if you do nothing to insinuate that you want to have sex with her.

6. Spoon in Bed

Many a couple spends their time lying in a spoon position at night, for the duration of slumber, or even in the morning, but now you're going to use such a position to your advantage. When you're lying behind her, tickle her neck with your lips and start kissing the area softly.

Of course, hopefully she will be responsive in a positive way (some women are very protective of their sleep time); but chances are, she won't complain.

What works even better is pressing your erection up against her behind. This lets her know that your mind's been wandering into the sexual realm and you want to satisfy your thoughts with her.

7. Morning Sex Interrupted

This is, by far, the most difficult tease to pull off because if she becomes incredibly responsive, you may not be able to hold back. And if she's not much of a morning sex kind of gal, then this will be impossible.

But for those of you who have lovely women who are good to go in the AM, wake up and give your stiffy a warm place to hang out for a while. The thing is that you have to practice *coitus interruptus* in this episode. When she begins to get extremely excited, pull out and ask her if she wants to continue.

She'll, of course, give you a resounding "yes!" You have to tell her that you will continue the fun, but at night when you get home from work. The fact that you can demonstrate such discipline, not to mention tease her so badly that she won't be able to think about anything else throughout the day, will definitely raise your greatest-man-in-the-world status through the stratosphere.

8. Blindfold Her

If she can keep her eyes closed while you do all the things that drive her crazy, then that will enhance the experience that much more. But since that's unlikely, it's highly recommended that you blindfold her.

This is your opportunity to do things you would otherwise be shy to do if she were watching. Use your tongue to lick up from her navel to the middle of her chest. Then stop and remove your body from hers completely. Make your way to her mouth and kiss her intensely.

By constantly removing yourself and striking in strategic areas of her body, the element of surprise will turn her on like crazy.

9. Make Your Way Inside

Although this might be a very difficult task for some, once you realize how much this drives her crazy, you'll want to keep it up forever. With her legs spread, welcoming you inside, take your time and allow only the tip of your penis to gently rub against her vaginal lips.

More likely than not, she'll begin rubbing herself on you trying to get you inside her—don't give in. When you see that she's about to go insane with desire, let only the tip of your penis enter her, and thrust in and out slowly.

If she says "faster," go slower, if she says "deeper," then stop altogether for a moment. The fact that you're not doing as she says will present her with a challenge and that's, ultimately, what you want.

Teasing women doesn't come naturally to most guys; it's a behavior that you must learn and practice. Be a challenge; don't give in when she makes it known that her juices are flowing.

Awaken all of her senses and your own by taking the time to drive her and yourself wild with desire. If you want to be her ultimate lover, taking things slowly will usually do the trick.

7 ORIGINAL PLACES TO TOUCH WOMEN

If you learn how to touch your woman in ways no man has ever touched her before, your chances of getting more sex from her will increase tenfold.

That said, here are seven parts of her body you might want to head to before you get your freak on. Not only will you arouse her immensely, you'll show her that you know that sex isn't simply about penetration.

1. Spine

While you should never massage the spine directly, feel free to use your tongue or fingers to glide up it every now and then. To drive her crazy, let your tongue graze over the little hairs on her back. Or, you can always use your fingers to tickle your way up to her neck.

2. Behind the Neck

The back of the neck is the spot that makes some women melt. Next time you kiss your girl, move her hair away from her neck (if applicable) and breathe on her neck, letting your lips graze against it before you kiss and then lightly bite into it.

3. Scalp

While you're kissing your girl, put your hands on the back of her head and massage her scalp for a minute. Feel free to give her hair a little tug from the roots; it will heighten her senses.

4. Shoulders

From kissing and massaging to lightly biting, the shoulders are an oft-ignored body part, but they should be given some serious attention. Because this area of a woman's body is often neglected, when you do spend some time appreciating her shoulders, she will get the chills and, in turn, you will get your thrills.

5. Breasts (not nipples)

We tend to instinctively head straight for the nipples and only grab on to the breasts when we want to bring the nipples closer to our mouths. However, if you want her nipple to beg for your attention, you need to spend some time kissing and caressing the surrounding area—the breast. Lick and bite near the nipples without actually touching them and she'll be begging you to wrap your mouth around them.

6. Outer Labia

As with the breast, when it comes to the vagina, we tend to dive right into the wet spot and ignore the outer lips. Assuming she's well groomed, use your mouth and tongue to lick and kiss the labia majora of your woman's vagina and when you finally head on in, she'll be soaked.

7. Ankles

It's somewhat anticlimactic to finish off with it, but some women love having their feet kissed and touched. But rather than her feet, opt to kiss and caress her ankles instead. Be careful; don't bite the area because it can hurt her.

5 FUN FOREPLAY POSITIONS

Foreplay isn't restricted to oral sex alone. Have a good time with other techniques that promote just touching—this can really help with arousal and build up to some wild sex later. Here are some creative foreplay positions to help you get hot 'n' heavy before jumping into a full-fledged, sheet-tangling, sweat-dripping showdown.

1. Nosedive

Description: She rests on her shoulders and raises her legs over your shoulders. You should place your hands under her bottom to give her added support. Here's a tip: Because this position can be strenuous on her back, she should lie with pillows under her shoulders.

NOSEDIVE

Benefits for you: The best thing about this position is the scenery—just look up and you'll get a pleasant view of her body from a great perspective. Since you have to support her legs, you also get easy access to her backside, so go ahead and cop a feel.

Benefits for her: Receiving oral sex at this angle can be quite pleasing for her, but it may be a little uncomfortable for her neck and shoulders. Take this position slowly and ask her how she's doing a couple of times, just to make sure she's enjoying it as much as you are.

2. Dairy Cow

Description: You're on all fours, while she lies on her back with her head directly beneath your groin area.

DAIRY COW

Benefits for you: This position is great for two reasons. First, you have the option of controlling the movement and the intensity of how she pleasures you. Second, if you're in the mood for it, you can "tea bag" her—that is, drop your scrotum into her mouth for some extra enjoyment.

Benefits for her: This position lets her be lazy. She can just lie back and give you a great ride without doing much at all. You can try to bring up this position if she's "too tired" or lacks the energy to perform oral sex.

3. Star 69

Description: In classic 69 form, you face each other's genitals for a great double oral sex session. In this position, she lies on the bottom and spreads her legs in the air, while you make your way on top of her.

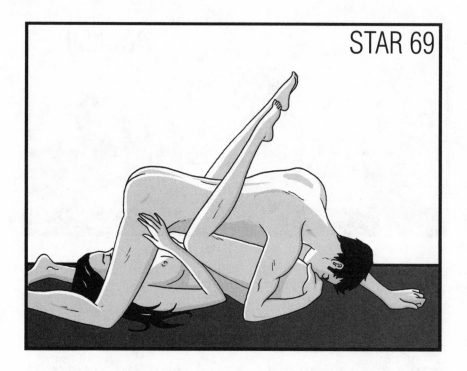

Benefits for you: As in "The dairy cow," you can control all motions and intensity according to what you like. Another rewarding thing about this position is that you have the option of using your fingers if your tongue starts to tire out.

Benefits for her: She gets to lie down—legs spread-eagled—and enjoy the ride. Pleasing you is simple through the magic of alignment—her head rests nicely under your groin area. Also, she has two options when it comes to using her free hands. She can either use them to caress herself, or she can use them on you for some extra pleasure.

4. Poolside

Description: While she lies on her stomach, you approach her from between her legs. Place a pillow under her stomach to give you easier access to her genitals.

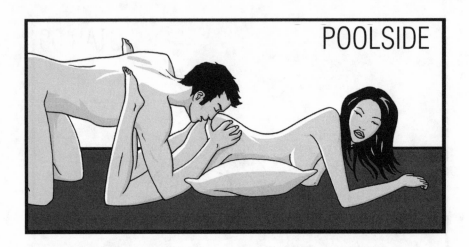

POOLSIDE

Benefits for you: You're in control here—use your hands, use just your fingers, use your tongue and your lips. Any way you do it, she's sure to enjoy the pampering.

Benefits for her: One of the great things about this position is the element of surprise—she can't really see you and has no idea what to expect. The "mystery" factor can lead to an overwhelming heightened sensation as she enjoys you enjoying her.

5. Electric Slide

Description: She leans on her side with one leg bent up and one stretched out; you lie on her outstretched leg, facing away from her. This position is great for caressing and massaging her legs and feet (and for getting yourself a little massage-action too).

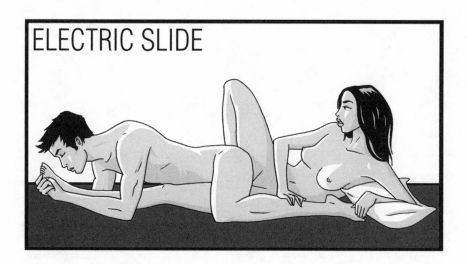

Benefits for you: This position is not only a relaxing, easy-going mutual foot massage technique. It leaves your backside exposed for her to caress, making anal stimulation a possibility if you'd like. Also, if you've got yourself a foot fetish, this is surely the way to go.

Benefits for her: Obviously, this is an ideal way to help her unwind and get into the mood. Hardly anyone can resist the sensuous charms of a relaxing rubdown.

RULE 7: LADIES FIRST

Men who dismiss foreplay as an intercourse element reserved "for her" need only reap its benefits once to change their tune. Focusing your foreplay techniques around optimizing her pleasure will do just that, bringing with it the associated benefits of increased frequency of intercourse and reciprocation: She'll devote equal time and attention to optimizing your pleasure.

Now, let's extend those benefits by carrying that lesson over to the later stages of intercourse. Our seventh rule will outline strategies and techniques for accommodating her both orally and in intercourse, optimizing her pleasure with an eye toward your own. From oral sex to her secret erogenous zones, we've compiled some of our best tips to help you rub her the right way.

GIVING HER ORAL PLEASURE—THE BASICS

We'll start our chapter on optimizing her pleasure with the basics of oral sex. From there, we'll progress toward more refined techniques.

Tongue to Lips

Were you aware that the tongue is the body's strongest muscle? Just imagine what you could do with your tongue if you were sexing her with it. Licking, sucking, and all-around moisture from the mouth to the vaginal entrance, the labia (lips) or the clitoris are surely going to make you popular with your flavor of the evening. Since you have more control with your tongue than with your penis, the sensations will drive her crazy.

Not only is your tongue naturally lubricated with saliva, it can maneuver itself in ways that a penis never could. So why not use your tongue to have sex with her?

■ Start off slowly . . . pretend that her entire vagina is a cherry lollipop and you've been dying to get a lick of it. Start by using your tongue to lick her vagina from her entrance up to her clitoris. Remember to chill out and relax—enjoy yourself and don't get tense.

■ Move your tongue freely from her inner lips to her outer labia on one side, whilst keeping all her lips inside your mouth. And since the other side will probably get jealous, move on to the other side afterwards.

■ Stick your tongue in and out, and when you're in, move your tongue around—*explore!*

■ Solidify your tongue at first and then allow it to soften, by relaxing your tongue muscles while licking her gently. Changing your cadence will keep her on her toes (or *off* as the case may be), wondering what your next move will be.

■ Don't be afraid to roam around, but remember to continuously return to her clitoris since most women's orgasms are clitoral—especially when it comes to cunnilingus.

■ Make sure not to apply too much pressure to her clitoris off the bat because it may irritate her and turn her off. Start out gently and, by reading her signals, increase pressure and speed accordingly.

When you've got her as hot as a lion in heat, the following techniques are going to drive her wild. Once again, make sure to pay attention to her reactions and body language at all times.

■ With her clitoris still exposed, give it quick little sucks by pulling it into your mouth momentarily and releasing it. This will definitely have a positive effect on her entire body.

■ Next, take her clitoris into your mouth and gently suck on it continuously whilst simultaneously flicking your tongue over and around it. You can perform this technique very lightly or aggressively, depending on what she likes.

■ There is nothing that a woman likes more than a multi-talented man, and if you know how to use both your tongue and fingers at the same time, you will definitely become the jack-of-all-trades. While you're French-kissing her clitoris, use your finger to rub it at the same time. Or, if you think that you can literally perform two different motions simultaneously, then whilst sucking on her clitoris, insert your finger(s) inside her and penetrate her vagina like a penis would.

■ Be careful not to lose sight of what you're doing because the vagina is a very shady, sensitive area, and one wrong move can leave you hanging out to dry. Keep up with what you're doing to her. Make sure that you're not thrusting your fingers too deep or too fast.

■ Use your tongue freely and don't be afraid to venture to uncharted territory; the more relaxed you are, the more relaxed she will be. And perhaps you weren't aware of this, but the feeling of your woman letting her juice flow all over your mouth is one of the world's greatest aphrodisiacs.

■ No one likes a slobbering idiot, so don't lose your mind while you're in her sacred garden. Don't start drooling all over her vagina and don't do random things—always have a plan when you're going down.

■ Lastly, and this can't be stressed enough, *don't bite any part of the vagina*. Not only can it cause physical harm, but you'll probably get thrown out of her house.

Useful Positions

In order to make your buffet as comfortable and as enjoyable as possible, have your lady lie on her back with her legs spread apart and her knees slightly bent. Lie on your stomach between her legs. Place both of your arms under her legs. Your head ends up comfortably facing your objective. Your arms wrap around her legs, which in turn, leave your hands free.

You can also sit in the same position and place both of your hands under her behind, propping it up so that it comes directly into your face. Although this requires a little more strength and requires both your hands, it can be very pleasurable for your woman.

Finally, you can have her lie down right at the edge of the bed, make her lie back, lift her feet to rest them on the edge of the bed as well, and you'll have plenty of access while you kneel in front of her love cave.

You are not restricted to these positions; there are plenty of other ones that guys can use to perform cunnilingus. Remember, don't be shy—experiment and have fun.

ULTIMATE ORAL SEX

Men like to believe that they're the kings of the bedroom-ring by trying all kinds of sexual positions. But when it comes time for oral sex, some men avoid performing it while others view it as a chore. This is where you can get an upper hand over the competition.

Because men don't value the power of good oral sex, they pay little attention to detail and fall short of creativity with their cunnilingus performance. 99% of men will perform oral sex in either one of two positions: with her lying on her back or in position number 69.

Oral sex is just as important as intercourse. Some women even find it more intimate than intercourse itself and reach orgasm more quickly via oral sex. If you want to be remembered as a great lover, you have to view oral sex as a main dish served in a variety of ways.

We all know the importance of foreplay before intercourse. But did you know that you too can join her list of unforgettable lovers by adding oral foreplay to your menu of tasty desserts?

Yes that's right! Don't jump onto her clitoris right away without first warming her up. Before you wind your tongue up, give her a teaser of what she can expect by taking your time to explore her erogenous zones.

During oral foreplay, use your tongue to lick her belly, inner thighs, behind her knees, her feet, her buttocks, and the area surrounding her genitals. You can use your lips to kiss her outer labia, but you can't use your tongue on her portal of pleasure. She knows that she'll eventually get the tongue, but never give it to her when she's expecting it.

Making her wait will increase her desire for you, but making her beg will ruin the mood. Stop the oral foreplay and give her what she desires at the right time. Observe the movement of her body. A dead giveaway is when your partner tries to position herself so that your mouth can find her. Creatively dive into her when she begins to press her inner thighs into you.

Anyone can perform regular oral sex, but for extraordinary sex, you need two important qualities: finesse and position variation.

1. Finesse:

Women don't like rough brutes, and they want to see that their men are enjoying themselves while performing oral sex. Show her that you enjoy eating her by taking your time and being gentle. Use your loving lips, tongue, and mouth on the areas surrounding her genitals.

When she can't stand it any longer, use your tongue as if it were a feather. Touch her vagina lightly, licking the labia and finding the vaginal opening. You can probe your tongue in and out, but remember, she's waiting for you to use your mouth.

Women's genitals are very sensitive. Don't bite, don't blow into her, and don't suck too hard. Everything you do has to be gentle; as if you're trying to lick a rose's petal without breaking it or pricking yourself.

When you feel the time is right, move on to her clitoris—what brings women to orgasm. Use your tongue to make slow, wide and sensual strokes from the vaginal opening to the clitoris.

Some men make the mistake of increasing the stroking speed once they sense the woman is close to orgasm. But this is not the right way. Instead, keep the same rhythm or even decrease the stroking speed of your tongue.

2. Position Variation:

Just like intercourse, oral sex feels different depending on how it's delivered. By trying different positions, oral sex can create different moods, result in different and exciting visual scenarios, and lead to different kinds of stimulation. This will, in turn, set you apart from other men and get her addicted.

Two different positions can really fuel a woman's orgasm: the Reverse Hug and the Doggy Greet.

Reverse Hug: This one is tricky but well worth it. You'll need to be in shape to do this, and it's another reason why you should exercise and build your muscles.

REVERSE HUG

Hold her upside down in front of you. Keep her head and shoulders resting on the bed, and her back resting against your stomach and chest. Hold her up, so that she won't feel too much pressure on the back of her neck. Have her wrap her legs around your head and lock her feet behind your neck. Wrap your arms around her belly and then simply lower your face between her legs.

Women enjoy this position because of the stimulation caused by the combination of oral sex and the "head rush" they may get when positioned upside down.

Doggy Greet: The Doggy Greet move involves a combination of doggy style intercourse and oral sex. This move requires a lot of control and willpower because you need to stop doing what feels best (penetrating her) so that you can concentrate on her pleasure.

DOGGY GREET

How do you do it? While having intercourse in the doggy position, pull out of her when you feel she is close to reaching orgasm. Then lower your head towards her flower and use your mouth and tongue with finesse as described above, until she reaches orgasm. Then just as she thinks the fun is over, enter her again with your manhood and I guarantee you she'll be very grateful for your unselfishness and creativity.

Why do women appreciate this move? Most women's favorite position is doggy style. It feels good but it becomes more or less predictable. The Doggy Greet is totally unexpected. Most women assume that a man cannot control himself and once penetration begins, a man won't stop until he is satisfied. By pulling out and giving her oral sex, you'll give her two different kinds of stimulation and show her your appreciation for her sexual needs.

Women like it when their men make sex exciting, adventurous, and spontaneous, and this includes oral sex. If you do it right, she will never let you go! You can have a small penis and still be brilliant sexually! It doesn't matter how gorgeous your face is, how big you are, or how built you are.

For women, any man who knows how to give great oral sex is worth his weight in gold! Give her the best possible oral sex and it's guaranteed you will get it back tenfold.

5 UNIQUE WAYS TO GO DOWN ON HER

While almost every woman will appreciate the classic cunnilingus positions like the muff dive and riding your face, you can bring her to the point of ecstasy by doing things no other man has done, or took the time to do.

Think of it this way: The average cunnilingus positions are just that, average. Do you want to be remembered as the average guy in bed? Didn't think so.

And remember, oral sex is a two-way street. The more time you go down on her, the more time she'll probably be spending on her knees.

When it comes to performing oral sex, try your best because she's going to talk to her friends about it. And you know what they say in the business world—the best advertisement is good "word of mouth."

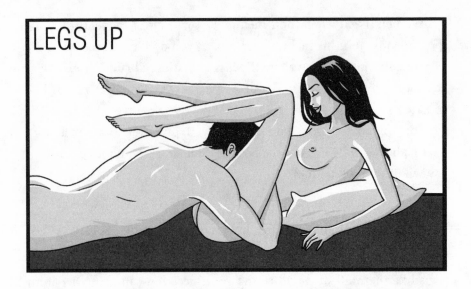

LEGS UP

1. Legs Up

This is just a slight variation of the basic "between her legs muff dive" that we all know and love. Have her start by lying on her back and putting her legs up over your shoulders. She may have to arch her back slightly to do this. You should be able to reach back and grab her ankles with your hands.

What you need to do: You want to position yourself between her legs. If you can easily reach back and grab her ankles with your hands, you're in the right position. If arching her back is the least bit uncomfortable for her, you should offer to get her a couple of pillows. Check her comfort level frequently at the appropriate times.

In this position, you have a full range of motion from the top of her vagina to the bottom. Try pulling her lips apart with your fingers very gently and licking the inside of her wall.

DIRTY DOGGY

2. Dirty Doggy

She should be on all fours with her butt up, facing away from you—exactly as she would if she were going to have sex with you in the doggy-style position.

What you need to do: Position yourself at a lower angle than her body, making sure your neck is comfortable. For example, put her on the bed with only her ass hanging over and you kneeling on the floor. This angle puts you in a great spot to rub your hands all over her backside. Encourage her to use whatever hand she is not bracing herself with to masturbate. And, gentleman, don't be afraid to lightly smack that booty.

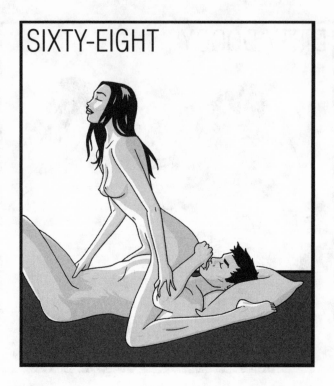

SIXTY-EIGHT

3. Sixty-Eight

This is built more for the girl who likes anal stimulation with a tongue, but you can also reach the lower part of her vagina. It's important to note that unless you have a tongue that could put Gene Simmons to shame, she will not get any sort of clitoral stimulation from this angle. You can, however, reach around with your hands and stimulate the clitoris and any part of the upper vagina with your hands.

What you need to do: Lie flat on your back on something comfortable. She will lie on top of you facing away (hence the term "68"). Take a deep breath and brace yourself for her weight. Make sure she has plenty of room for her legs and arms.

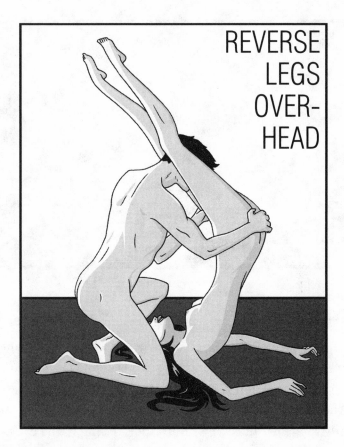

REVERSE LEGS OVER-HEAD

4. Reverse Legs Overhead

Have her begin by laying flat on her back with her legs straight out. Next, help her swing her legs up and over her head to where her legs are facing in the opposite direction. She will basically be in the same position she would use if she were stretching out her back in yoga class.

What you need to do: Position yourself near her head and shoulder area, kneeling down with one leg. At this spot you can easily slide your middle fingers inside of her and are at the perfect angle to hit her G-spot. With her ass that high in the air you can also gently stimulate the anus at the same time you are down on her.

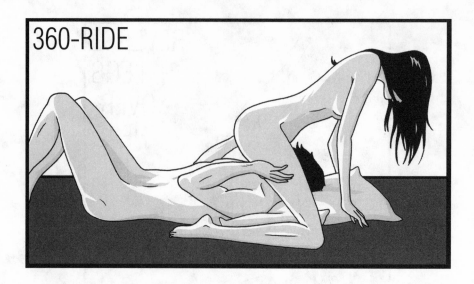

5. 360-Ride

This will begin with her riding your face for a brief while, and is followed by her gently rotating her hips/pelvis around your face until she is in the opposite direction that she started (making a whole 180-degree turn). After a few moments with you down on her in this position, she will gently rotate her hips/pelvis until she is facing in the direction she started (completing a 360-degree turn).

This position will give her more control and she is ultimately responsible for the speed, pressure, and where your tongue is going.

What you need to do: Find a comfortable spot where you can lie flat on your back. Be sure to have your head facing something like a headboard that she can grab onto, making the turns much easier for her. Be sure to protect your face when she is turning or the sudden shift in weight could seriously damage your nose.

In the beginning of this position, your hands will be free to manually get yourself off. She'll get the idea that going down on her can get you off as a huge compliment. However, be sure to focus more attention on her than on your own personal hand job, or she may feel you are more into your needs than hers.

On the flip side, when she completes the first 180-degree turn, her hands are free to complete what you started.

---

10 UNEXPECTED FEMALE EROGENOUS ZONES

As curiosity is part of our genetic makeup, most men remain curious as to what turns a woman on. What spot can we touch to drive her absolutely crazy?

While it doesn't take a rocket scientist to discover men's erogenous zones (the penis, the testicles, and the anus), women get aroused through very diverse body parts. Ah women, what an exquisite species! Let's get started on our journey through a woman's body, shall we?

10. Inner Thighs

The inside of the thighs are highly sensitive to touching, stroking, and licking. Just like the back of the knees, inner thighs also have many nerve endings, therefore when you fondle them, you will turn her on like crazy.

Remember not to bite because the area is very sensitive and doing so would only cause her mild pain, which will, in turn, cause you plenty of pain.

9. Behind the Knees

Because of all the nerve endings behind the knees, you'd be surprised at how crazy a woman can become when you gently lick or nibble on the back of her knees.

Be careful not to overdo it—the area, after all, is very sensitive and you must be careful not to make the sensation annoying by getting too rough or tickling her too much.

8. Buttocks

Yes, it's true. Lots of women like it when you play around with their be-hinds. A lot of women like mild spanking and squeezing of the buttocks. But there's more . . .

Some women like having their butts licked, sucked, and penetrated (with fingers, penis, or both). For those who shudder at the thought of sticking their tongues out at Uranus, I'm sure that anal penetration, on the other hand, sounds quite inviting, huh?

7. Nape of the Neck

Just breathing on this part of her body will give her goose bumps all over. So just imagine her reaction when you use your tongue or teeth to get her aroused.

Use your hands too; lift her hair up gently as you bring your mouth closer to her neck. Then, as you sink your teeth into it, pull on her hair slightly so as to give that "I want you sooo bad" impression.

This part of a woman's body is also a good place to start giving her that sensual massage you are famous for and no woman can resist.

6. Ears

Many women enjoy having their ears licked, sucked, or kissed. Although blowing in her ear is acceptable, it's not what women enjoy most. Also, women like it when you whisper in their ears.

Don't whisper things like, "Can you wash my gym shorts tonight?" Try to be somewhat erotic and give her the shivers up and down her spine instead.

5. Feet

Many women enjoy having their feet touched and massaged, and some even enjoy having them licked and sucked. Assuming that their feet have been properly cleaned, women enjoy it when their men spend time caressing their soles, toes, and ankles. Because these zones can all be ticklish, the sensation of ticklishness can be pleasant for the recipient.

While some men cringe at the thought of wrapping their mouths around a body part that spends most of its day sweating in leather, many guys are actually pretty keen on the idea of giving their women a good toe lashing every now and then.

4. Wrists

This may come as a shock to most guys, but women love having their wrists nuzzled and nibbled by their lovers. The next time you're getting into the foreplay of things with your woman, begin kissing and caressing her wrists and just check out how impressed and turned on she'll become!

3. Breasts (Nipples)

It's surely no surprise to anyone that the breasts are very sexually sensitive, and that gentle fondling, squeezing, caressing, licking, and sucking of the nipples can be extremely arousing.

Just as well, many women like it when their guys get a little rough with their little mountains, so find out how she likes it and give it to her the way she wants!

2. Vagina/Clitoris

The clitoris can be stimulated by using the tongue, the finger or, for the multi-talented Joe, both simultaneously. Some women like to guide their lovers as to the specific amount of pressure they enjoy.

For those who don't get that luxury, it's usually quite evident whether or not she's pleased with your performance. If she begins getting squirmy, make sure that it's because she's enjoying it and not because you're giving her that "annoying" feeling.

And the number one female erogenous zone . . .

1. Lips

Yes, it's true. If you know how to manipulate her lips just right through kissing, licking, sucking, and biting, it is very possible that a kiss will lead to a lot more than that. Use your lips, your tongue, and your teeth to play with her top and bottom lip and kiss her with absolute passion.

HOW TO BUY HER A SEX TOY

You've demonstrated your selflessness to her in your foreplay, oral, and intercourse techniques. Now it's time to take your sexual generosity to the next level by indulging her in a gift that clearly designated for her enjoyment: a sex toy. Buying a woman a sex toy is a bold move, and there is a large margin of error if you are not careful. Giving her a huge double-ended dildo with five differently shaped attachments will probably scare her to death, while a fake tongue may gross her out. And if you give her a life-sized male blow-up doll, forget it—she'll probably dump you.

If you want to surprise her and not have it backfire on you, read on. Here's how to make finding it, buying it, and giving it to her a much more seamless and pleasurable process.

The easiest way to know what she would like is to ask her, but if you are buying her a surprise gift, you will have to make an educated guess.

Whatever your woman's overall preferences, they are likely to vary with her mood, so you need to choose a toy that will suit the range of her aroused occasions. Your safest bet is to buy something that provides pleasure to all zones at various speeds that offer different levels of pressure.

Finding and Buying It

If you choose to go into a "real" sex shop, you can get some great advice from the shop staff; they breathe in latex fumes and discuss the most lewd and interesting topics all day long; they know what they are talking about so don't be shy. The people in these stores are great at making you feel comfortable, and it's better to go in and discuss your purchase with someone who works there than to walk around clumsily looking for something you've never seen before. Shopping for sex toys online is also a safe bet and it saves embarrassment because it is discreet.

Don't Forget the Lube

Sex toys are generally easier to use and more pleasurable when used with lube, so make sure to invest in some good quality water or silicon-based lube for your girl when you buy her the toy.

Bigger Is Not Better

When buying a phallic dildo or vibrator for a girl, don't just assume that bigger is better. On the scale of things, most women prefer to masturbate with something very penis-like in length, girth, and texture, if not smaller, like the popular "lady finger" vibe.

If you do not know her too well and are guessing what she will like, stay on the safe side and avoid huge double-ended dildos, strap-ons, and anything anal. The safest bets are to keep it to well-known erogenous zones.

Silicon, Rubber, Metal, or Glass

You don't want to go overboard with the first sex toy; keep this one simple, subtle, and functional. Silicon and rubber have the most life-like feel to them and are always a good choice. They are also very safe, and warm up under a hot tap easily.

Metal is a bad choice because it is quite cold to start off with, though its firmness may be the selling point. Metal can look quite attractive too, and since sex toys aren't the most gorgeous things on earth, it's a plus if they're not ugly.

There are some very beautiful glass dildos available. Glass offers a very smooth sensation, and can be cooled or heated to give her some variety.

Opting for the "Joe-blow average" toy is your best bet. Stick to the basics. If in doubt, go with silicon. Silicon is neither too soft nor too hard and is durable and hygienic, making it an excellent choice for sex toys.

Do your homework. Going with the best-selling or most popular toy is normally a good choice if you are flooded with a gazillion toys that all look the same.

Quality vs. Cost

Don't scrimp and save on this toy because you want quality. Having a toy not work or fall to bits at the crucial moment is going to make you look like a cheapie—a mortal sin in chick-talk!

Presenting It to Her

There are a number of ways to do this. If you want it to be a surprise gift, the classiest thing you can do is have it wrapped and posted straight to her with a sexy note. If you want to use it with her, you could put it under the pillow and give it to her on the spur of the moment, though this approach could have negative consequences if, for some reason, she has a problem with your purchase.

If you have any doubt about the reception you will receive, opt for the safety of the shore: Warn her, and give it to her in a non-sexual situation so she doesn't feel pressured or uncomfortable. Make it funny or sexy—in other words, make it special in some way. It is highly likely that upon receiving your thoughtful and sexy gift, she will not be able to stop smiling and giggling.

She'll Turn It On and Get Turned On

Buying your girlfriend a sex toy doesn't have to be a traumatizing experience. Finding a good shop, whether online or downtown, makes life a lot easier: The staff will be educated, the packaging will be discreet, and the toy will go the distance and handle the punishment dished out to it. It takes balls for a man to buy his woman a sex toy without her input, so give yourself a pat on the back for being so brave and courageous. Let her enjoy the fruits of your labor, and let yourself enjoy the fruits of her pleasure.

RULE 8: LOCATION

Sex can happen anywhere, anytime. But it can also become same old, same old. Whether you're suddenly overcome with passion, or you're looking for a little something new to break the monotony, a change of scene will often do the trick. Whether it's the backseat, the shower, on a mountaintop, or in an airplane washroom, there's nothing like a variety of new and exciting locations to spice up your sex life.

THE BEST PLACES TO HAVE SEX

Are you tired of engaging in run-of-the-mill sex in your bedroom, on your bed, day in and day out? Well, the tips that follow are going to sway you away from the everyday and reveal some common and some not-so-common spots where you and your beautiful babe can engage in the nasty.

Before beginning, keep in mind that striving to constantly outdo the place before will get quite boring fast, so make sure to reserve these places for those kinky mood moments or those "I need to get inside you" times.

Backseat: Yes, most of us have prodded or will prod at least one woman in the backseat (or front seat) of our cars. Okay, so it may not be the roomiest of spots and perhaps the knee burns will last for days, but hey, it'll be a fond memory once you get all the stains out of the upholstery.

You don't necessarily have to take her into the backseat and start banging away like a hammer against a nail. Rather bring her to some remote area, kiss her softly from across the driver's seat, slowly inching your hand up her thighs.

You can spend the entire time teasing her with your mouth and fingers, or you can lead her to the backseat and get busy. Make sure to wear easy access clothing though, or the whole thing might end up getting sloppy and non-mood inducing.

Hotel: Bring her to a new destination, and hence a new room other than yours or hers. You can prepare the hotel room beforehand with oils, candles and the like, or you can just go get the hotel room together.

The great thing about getting a room for the night is that you can make the biggest mess and get nasty all night long without having to worry about the mess the morning after. You can literally spill candle wax everywhere, soak the carpet, let your little buddies soak into the bed (who gets the wet spot?), and all that other good stuff that would otherwise be an annoying mess for one of you to clean up.

The best thing to do is plan this kind of evening when there's no special occasion; do it just for a change in scenery. She will be thrilled at the prospect of making love in a new environment and you'll reap the benefits. Unleash the sexual demons.

Hot Tub: Unless you're living large, most of us can only fit one person into our bathtub comfortably. A hot tub, on the other hand, allows for parties of two (or more).

The roominess that a hot tub has, as well as that vibrating jet streaming action, will ultimately make you and your partner lose yourselves in the moment, among other things . . .

You can be naked, in boxers, or even in swimming trunks (leave the g-string for her please), and she . . . well she should be naked from the get go (kidding, but it is highly recommended). Remember that your aim here is to make this moment tub-full of memories.

Waterbed: Many claim that the waterbed should be the world's one-stop shop for bed sex. Why? Well, simply because if you can get the perfect flow and go with the rhythm (against the wave), then it can be absolutely mind blowing.

What's even better is removing the bed sheets and having just the water mattress exposed. Slather it, as well as yourselves, with baby oil and have fun slipping and sliding everywhere–including inside of her.

This doesn't require the likes of a mathematical genius and hey, hopefully no one will get seasick from the motion of the sexual ocean. Just imagine all the fun you can have.

Sauna: What makes sex in a sauna so absolutely, incredibly, mind-blowingly amazing? How about the fact that because you're blocking some oxygen from getting to the brain (via the lack of oxygen), your senses become heightened and thus every thrust, lick, and bite is felt in an exaggerated manner.

Imagine walking into a hot, wet room with your woman and the both of you are wearing nothing but towels? Come on, that alone sounds erotic. Hopefully, the two of you will have reserved the sauna for yourselves; that way, you can let go completely and get crazy on one another.

Private office party: If you have the keys to your office, then why not bring her to work and show her how hard you work on your desk? Perhaps it's the element of danger or the fact that it's taboo that arouses people so easily when it comes to the idea of engaging in a sexual romp at their workstations.

One night, blindfold your woman and bring her to the office. Don't tell her where you're taking her and once there, don't reveal where you are. Undress her slowly and savor every moment so that the next time you go to work, you can remember every second of the session.

In the midst of making love to her, remove the blindfold, let her see her surroundings and start thrusting yourself in and out of her with every ounce of passion you have in you—pour it all into her.

In the club: Taking your woman out on the town should be a given as it is, but why not plan a night of dancing at a local nightclub? Let her don her sexiest outfit and take her to the club where the two of you will drink, dance, and be merry.

Soon after, lead her to the washroom, preferably the men's room as there's hardly lineups and men have urinals. Take her into the stall and start ravishing her with kisses and grope her body as though it's the first time you're looking at her.

Your best bet is to opt for the doggy position, as it'd probably be the most comfortable if you want to do your thing discreetly. Otherwise, let her hold onto the top of the stall with both hands above the toilet. She can wrap her legs around your waist and you can ram her till the cows come home. Or at least, until the bouncer puts an end to your bouncing.

Beach: Yes, perhaps it is a cliché, but nevertheless, the beach does have that certain flair. Even just saying, "We had sex on the beach" sounds amazing. Come on, they even named a drink after it—it's *that* good.

Prepare the night; get a bottle (or two) of wine, some munchies (grapes, crackers, cheese), a blanket, and whatever else you need, and head for that sandy sexual playground. Don't hop on top of her the second you arrive—chill out and enjoy what the moment has to offer.

As the evening progresses, the surroundings alone might get her in the mood.

4 LOCATIONS FOR A QUICKIE

Time is of the essence, but you and your girl want to find a spot where you can get a couple of quick pumps in before you have to get back to whatever it is you were going to do. Here, now, are seven places where you might want to consider grinding into your girl the next time your blood runs heavy below the waist.

■ *Elevator*

You might try to stall the elevator (given that you don't trigger any alarms by doing so, unless you enjoy getting caught), penetrate, and when you're done and let the elevator run again, don't exit from the main floor.

Ideal position: Upright wheelbarrow (with her facing the wall, hold her up by her thighs, placing them on either side of your hips, while she holds on to the wall).

■ *Stairwell*

If your roommate's home, or you and your girlfriend only have 10 minutes to spare for a lunch date, head to the stairwell of a building with an elevator, preferably on a really high floor, and go crazy for a few minutes.

Ideal position: Missionary, with her back arched over a stair.

■ *Alley*

Before you begin envisioning rats and drunks, picture an alley behind a restaurant that isn't as filthy as those you see in movies. Ideally, she'd be wearing a skirt and the both of you could head to an alleyway just after dinner and before the show. Now *that's* an intermission.

Ideal position: Standing up, with one leg wrapped around you.

■ *Dressing Room*

How many times has your girl got you all hot and bothered while she's changing in the dressing room of a clothing store? Well, why not add some kick to the tedious task of shopping by sneaking into the changing room with her and giving her a little taste of your dressing?

Ideal position: Standing Doggy.

GEAR UP FOR CAR SEX

Why is having sex in a car so common among couples? To start, it's because there's nothing more thrilling than the thought that you might get caught doing the nasty. Not to mention, car sex is spontaneous and, of course, everyone feels the need to fulfill the "we did it in a car" cliché.

But besides clinging onto your youth and engaging in some naughty fun in your ride, sex in a car is much cheaper than renting a hotel, or a motel, for that matter. So just about everyone has engaged in sex via car, and although you're in the car for the main event, what locale will you go to in order to reap the most fun for the least worry?

In every city and in every town, there is that one spot that all the young folks go to for the sole purpose of making out (among other things), but do you really want to take your woman to "The Point"? Of course not, you want to take her elsewhere for your sexual endeavors.

Parking Lots

If both of you are the more daring type, then a parking lot can serve as a wonderful area to get sweaty and nasty. Of course, you'll likely fog up the windows, but don't fret, everyone will know what you're up to.

Drive-in Movie

Sure, this is the mother of all clichés, but really, how many people are still having sex at the drive-in theater? So plan it in your head without letting her know, get her to wear something that provides easy access and enjoy the movie.

Back Alley

No, this is not the prelude to one of your perverse dreams. If your woman isn't very thrilled with having an audience, taking her to a very quiet and preferably dark area will serve you better. Opt for an alley that people rarely, if ever, frequent.

Mountaintop

There's nothing quite like watching the sunset (or rise) and penetrating the woman you love at the same time. Drive to the top of a mountain (given that you don't live in the flatlands) and make slow, quiet love for as long as it takes to satisfy each other.

Positions

Of course, assuming that your car is somewhat roomier than a sub-sub-sub compact, there are a variety of positions you can enjoy in the comfort of your own automobile.

Doggy Dash

Sit on the passenger side and tilt the passenger seat back as much as you can. She can sit on top of you facing the windshield, holding onto the dashboard for balance and controlling the movement. And what a movement it is—not too mention that awesome view of her backside.

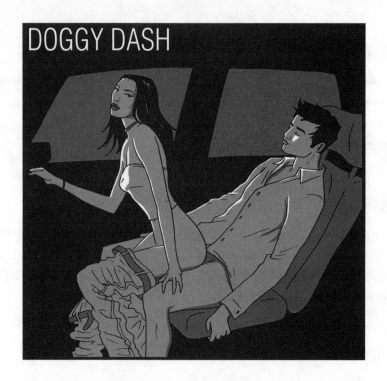

Backseat Mission

There really isn't much to this position. You basically go in the back with your woman and take your place as the missionary man. For a little variety, try to raise her legs so that the soles of her feet rest on the ceiling of the car. And don't be shy; give her little portal a kiss hello.

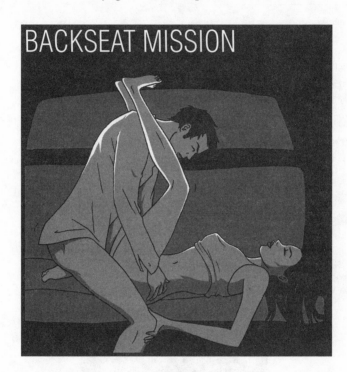

BACKSEAT MISSION

Lighthouse

You need to have a sunroof for this oldie but goodie. Stand with your feet on the driver's seat and while your woman sits in the comfort of the passenger seat, she can pleasure your manhood while you keep a lookout for undesirables.

Hoodlicker

If you and your woman are bold, then place her on the hood of your car and enjoy all the treats she has to offer. Of course, when she's ready to take you in, you can turn her over and let her hands rest on the hood while you penetrate her.

Helpful Tips

Music: The sound track can make or break the experience. Make sure you have some appropriate tunes on hand.

Parking brake: Believe it or not, many people forget all about this simple little action. It's very important to ensure that the parking brake is on, otherwise you may just end up naked in a ditch, and no one wants that.

Clean car: Any woman would be apprehensive about removing her clothes and getting down in a car that has McDonald's wrappers on the floor or a sticky dash. Make sure the inside of your car is spotless.

Fog windows: Turn off the air conditioning and make sure that the windows get fogged up before you pull up her skirt and give her your greeting.

Easy-access clothing: Make sure that you're wearing clothes that can be removed and put on easily. The last thing you want to do is knee her in the face while trying to pull down your fitted jeans.

Baby wipes: How many times do people get caught naked in their cars without tissues to wipe up? Make sure you have baby wipes handy to clean up the mess you'll be making.

Be prepared: Remember that sex in the car is not approved of in most parts, so make sure you're in a position that you can easily get dressed in. Mr. Police Officer doesn't need to know whether or not your woman shaves or waxes down there.

5 WAYS TO GO BEYOND THE BEDROOM

Expand your sexual terrain needn't require leaving the house. There are plenty of instantly accessible props and locales within your residence that can help ramp up your sex life.

1. Put Her on the Washer

Somehow the rumor got started that the vibrations of the washing machine make women orgasm. Whether or not this is true isn't as important as the fact that women seem to find the sensation agreeable, so why not give it a try? Maybe someday an enterprising company will make a washer with a seat on top especially for this purpose.

2. Go on the Roof

The element of danger or of being seen can make this quite exciting. If possible, climb out there on a warm, quiet night, bring a bottle of wine and a blanket and start out with a mini picnic. If you don't have roof access, you can bring a blanket out to the balcony and have sex there instead.

3. Have Sex in the Bathroom

The bathroom is the perfect place to get some privacy, and there are dozens of ways to position her for sex here. You can look at her in the mirror while you penetrate her from behind, you can prop her up on the sink, or you can sit on the toilet while she rides you. And no mention of the bathroom would be complete without bringing up the shower. We'll explore this venue in more detail later.

4. Kitchen/Dining Room Table

This is an age-old place to have sex in the house. It's popular for a reason: it's a firm, flat surface that can hold your weight. You can make use of the chairs and the table; just clear it off first.

5. Turn Out All the Lights

Hindering eyesight can lead to bolder sexual behavior. Shut off every light in the house, put on a glow-in-the-dark condom, and play hide and seek.

And while the lights are out you can do an unlimited amount of other kinky sex acts. Sexual novelty companies also make a surprising array of glow-in-the-dark products like bubble baths, panties, handcuffs, dildos and vibrators, massage lotions, and body paint.

This is just a sampling of the many ways you can spice up your sex life around the house. There are a million variations on this theme. Sometimes, the smallest thing, such as a different room or the use of a mundane object can turn a vanilla sex life into one that incorporates every flavor in the book.

8 WAYS TO LOVE HER IN THE SHOWER

So, you and your lover have conquered every other domain of your house: the bedroom, the living room, the rec room, the laundry room, the kitchen table, the kitchen counter tops. Now what? Or rather, where?

Well, one of the most likely places to find her in the buff and halfway ready is the bathroom. You can keep your lovemaking fun and playful by leading her into the bathroom, or you can surprise her by jumping into the shower to help her with the cleansing experience. Either way, you better make sure the tub is scrubbed; nothing can turn a woman off faster than soap rings and mildew.

While she's out, clean the toilet. Then place plenty of scented candles around the bathroom: on the closed toilet, on the sink, on the shelves, on the rim of the tub, everywhere, to give the bathroom a nice romantic glow. Draw a hot bath and add some nice bath oils once it's filled. Next—and no, it's not a waste—scatter some rose petals into the bath and let some fall to the floor as well. Stay away from incense. There will be enough aromas from the candles and oils and there is no need to pollute the air with smoke.

When she returns from her stressful day, invite her to join you in this sanctuary.

For practical purposes, we have limited this list to water sports in the conventional, bathtub/shower combination found in most homes and apartments.

As with most sports, there are safety issues. With water sports in the shower, the key issues are footing and lube. Take precautions: water tends to dry up natural lubrication, so be sure that you are prepared with some lube from the shop. Also, footing is an issue. You need footing to properly give thrust, so you might want to invest in those adhesive grips for the bottom of the tub. Be safe and have fun.

LEG LIFT

1. Leg Lift

This position allows for the couple to face each other. She leans her back against the wall while you hold her knee in the crook of your elbow. Depending on height, as you are probably taller than your partner, initial penetration may be an issue. At first, you should bend at the knees to gain access. Also, if you both want to enjoy the falling water it is best for the female to lean against the wall with the showerhead.

STANDING DOGGY

2. Standing Doggy

In this position, the female bends over and clutches the rim of the tub. Her knees should be slightly bent to maintain balance and to absorb some shock. You should hold onto her hips, and occasionally caress her body (along her spine, her abs, her breasts). Again, if you both want to enjoy the water, the female should be facing the faucets. This allows the water to fall on the small of her back and hit your lower torso. The steady stream of water on your genitals will feel amazing.

3. Standing Doggy (alternate)

In this position, she stands facing a wall with her arms raised and pressed against it. Her lower back will have to be arched, thrusting her butt towards you. You can get up close and hold her hands against the wall or you can hold her hips. If you decide to hold her hips, balance becomes your responsibility and you might want to place a foot on the edge of the tub.

4. Oral Obsession

Since you're both clean and fresh, why not take advantage of it and please each other orally. Either one of you could drop to your knees to please the other, but unlike dry land, you can't put a pillow under your knees to make the experience more comfortable. The person receiving should stand on the edge of the tub, holding onto the shower rod with one hand and the wall with the other for balance. The person giving may have to bend slightly, but at least they aren't on their knees. This technique also lends itself to an incredible amount of access to the lower regions. Two points of caution: don't fall and don't drown.

5. Moving Mountains

The shower definitely lends itself to the opportunity; hopefully your girl is up and down for it too. You have plenty of water and plenty of soapy lube, so go for it. After her breasts and your member are all lathered you're pretty much set. With the palms of her hands placed on the external portion of her breasts, she pushes towards the middle of her chest; her fingers make a bridge across the crevice to keep your member contained below.

You might have to try a couple of different positions to decide which you like best. She can go down low, providing a steady place for you or you can go up high, standing on the edge of the tub once again. The advantage of being up high is that she can provide a little more movement and it is more comfortable for all.

6. Manual Manipulation

She likes it. She likes seeing you masturbate. It turns her on. So get over yourself and enjoy it. You can do it solo (each of you enjoying the sight of your partner getting off) or you can do one another.

There is a lot you can do in this department, but it's highly recommend that you invest in a detachable massage showerhead. Lube up her butt cleavage, stand behind her and place your package in that cleavage. Use one of your hands to caress her breasts and with the other, aim the showerhead at her clitoris. Let her fingers do their magic.

7. Back-door Fun

The shower, with all its cleansing power, lends itself to the possibility of anal adventures actually happening. If you've ever encountered the excuse, "I don't feel clean enough," or "I haven't prepared for this," then the shower has become your new best friend. Of course, no matter how you propose this, the decision is all hers. Just try to present it as a fun thing and don't appear too desperate or you might run the risk of getting nothing at all.

Try one of the standing doggy styles.

8. Take a Break on the Edge

We all love it when she takes control of the movement. Take a seat on the edge of the tub and let her lower herself onto you, with her back to you. You'll have to hold the edge of the tub for balance (you can't hold her or you will interrupt her movement). She will have to support herself on your knees with her hands and she will have to use her arms and legs to move herself up and down.

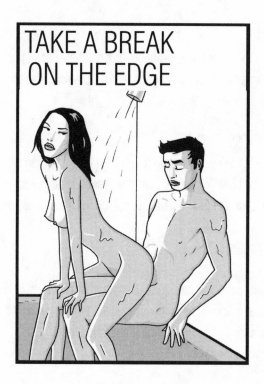

TAKE A BREAK
ON THE EDGE

7 PUBLIC PLACES FOR SEX

Feel like upping the risk factor a bit, and her arousal levels with it? Try slipping in a quickie at one of these locales.

The Shopping Mall

Just wait for the shoppers to look the other way and duck inside a "Mall Personnel Only" door. And because those back walkways are so quiet, it's easy to hear footsteps approaching.

Empty University Classroom

Schools usually post a schedule of when each room is free and when it's in use. Just take note of an opportune time and show up. Universities being trusting types, these rooms often remain open.

The Park

A spot deep in the woods is probably no good because of poison ivy, deer ticks, and an assortment of other hazardous plants and creatures. So find a hidden grassy spot somewhere out of sight.

On a Downtown Train

If you find yourselves on a train for an hour or so, find an empty train car and get busy. Look for the cars with the bench seats; plush upholstery is preferable. Just wait until the train is not too full and it's nearing the end of the line.

Cemetery

It's deserted, peaceful, and quiet. Usually the front gate is always open, but if not, it should still be relatively easy to get in. The most you'll have to do is jump a fence. Just wait until after nightfall.

Golf Course

The grass is manicured and soft. And because there are probably not going to be any twigs, branches, or rocks, you may not even need a blanket! It's best to go for a public golf course because country clubs are a little touchier about trespassing.

Coat Check

Just duck inside, quietly close the door (if there is one) and get down to business. Even if someone comes in to get their coat, if the room is somewhat big, they probably won't be wise to a thing.

More women are turned on by sex in public than you might think. And it makes you look like a spontaneous, fun guy, which is always a good image to cultivate.

There are limitless places you can take her for a quickie, as long as you've got a plan. Remember: it's all about the right timing. So don't let anyone sneak up on you or it'll be the last time she tries it.

JOINING THE MILE HIGH CLUB

Okay, you've heard about the Mile High Club. You could say it's like taking public sex to another level, with all the increased titillation that comes with. Of course, the mile high club has an air of legitimacy because this particular type of public sex already has its own club name.

What is the mile high club? The self-proclaimed "official site of the mile high club" has defined it as "two people engaging . . ." in sexual activity (sexual intercourse) at an altitude of no less than 5,280 ft (a mile high above the earth) in an airplane."

Do It in Private

Some people actually do it sitting in their seats, either angling to the side and penetrating from behind, or even with the woman sitting on the guy's lap. Problem is, both positions are fairly obvious to those around, or if the plane is relatively empty, to the flight attendants, since they're devoting more of their attention to you. The bathroom, although cramped, is private, and therefore preferable. After all, you're not committing a crime. Better to experience the satisfied embarrassment of getting caught leaving the bathroom together than to be caught in mid act.

Techniques & Positions

If doing it in a bathroom, obviously a first-class bathroom is slightly easier. Regardless, your position choices are pretty limited:

- fellatio, her seated, you standing
- cunnilingus, her standing on seat, you crouching in front of it
- penetration from behind
- penetration, her sitting on sink edge, you standing
- penetration, standing missionary (if she's taller than you)

Sit Near a Bathroom

Many people plan to do this together as a shared "high," if you will. If you're going to plan this, perhaps try to sit near a bathroom, either at the back of the plane or, on a bigger plane, near the bulkhead and away from the kitchen, to lower your chances of getting caught entering.

Head to the Bathroom Separately

Do so, obviously, when there is no line-up. Make a knock signal so that, to others in the plane who have forgotten there's someone already in the bathroom, it looks like you're simply knocking to ensure it's empty before entering.

Get Busy While Passengers Are Sleeping

Try to time your actions for when most passengers are sleeping. A red-eye flight is ideal. The end of the in-flight movie is obviously not.

Wear Loose Clothes

If planning ahead, you should wear easily removable clothing for easy access.

RULE 9: ADAPT TO HER

Awoman is a unique, beautiful creature—no two are quite the same. And it follows that you must treat each woman as an individual, and attune yourself to her particular needs and desires. It could be the time of the month, a lack of confidence on her part, a difference in age or experience, or maybe she's on the rebound. Whatever the circumstance, be sensitive and do your best to understand her. She'll find your attention incredibly sexy, guaranteed.

HOW A WOMAN'S CYCLE AFFECTS HER LIBIDO

Would you like to be able to predict the dates when a woman is most likely to be gagging for it? Believe it or not, it's entirely possible. All it takes is a little bit of research, a calendar, and some careful observation, and you will be well on your way to making the most of nature's erotic gifts (and have a much higher chance of knowing when to keep out of the stomping zone of a wild premenstrual woman).

It is proven beyond reasonable doubt that a woman's sexual desires increase dramatically during (and just after) ovulation. In that light, let's look at the best times for sex and how men can make the most of a woman's high times.

When Is the Best Time to Get It On?

The short answer is during ovulation, when a woman is at her most fertile. The longer answer, which involves what ovulation is and how to pinpoint when it's happening, is as follows.

What Is Ovulation?

Ovulation is the process of a healthy egg arriving in the uterus, ready for fertilization. When the egg is in the perfect place for fertilization, the woman's body sends her libido into overdrive. This is the only time during the month that she is fertile, and there is only a 12- to 24-hour period in which she can actually get pregnant. The hormones produced at this time mean she is extra sensitive in all her senses—especially in smell and touch.

Why Ovulation Is Good for You

It is no coincidence that one-night stands often end in pregnancy. Ovulation is when the body says "Get me pregnant!" At other times, it is not as necessary for the body to encourage copulation. This is when you can predict her behavior reasonably; her body ensures this by being the lovely regular thing it is. (Of course, not every woman has a regular cycle, but most do.) She is much more likely to say yes if she is ovulating. This is good for you. It is important to stress the fertility part of this equation: Her body is doing its damnedest to get her pregnant, so watch out! Unless you are ready for fatherhood, of course . . .

When Does Ovulation Occur?

Because every woman has a slightly different cycle—some women have 20 days and others have 60 days—it is not that easy to pinpoint the exact day of ovulation. It is 14 to 16 days *before* the first day of her period, *not* 14 to 16 days *after* her period (unless she has a perfectly even 28-day cycle). The number of days before and after her period may be uneven; it is not strictly halfway.

What's Going Through Her Head While She Is Ovulating?

It is during ovulation that women find themselves gripped in the midst of a craving for sex with attractive men. "Attractive" is always in the eye of the beholder, of course, and standards during this time tend to drop significantly. The craving for penetrative sex with a live man (as opposed to going solo with a motorized "friend") can be overwhelming. The desire for a romp with a warm masculine body is intense and, very often, irresistible.

Ovulating women often put themselves out there a little more, feeling and behaving in a more provocative and flirty manner despite their best intentions. This time of a woman's cycle is biologically very different from the rest, in that her sexuality becomes a flashing neon light that says: "Fertility." She feels sexy, she feels desirable, she feels the energy of her womanhood bubbling to the surface.

Sex During Her Period

Most women experience a rise in their sex drive during their period. This is inconvenient timing, and you will find that some women will not want to have sex in this time despite their desire to do so because of the intimate difficulties that arise. For example, if she is wearing a tampon, removing it can leave her vagina dry, and it can take a long time to moisten up with natural lubricant (not blood). If she is wearing a pad, she may feel embarrassed about the smell of her vagina and the immediate presence of blood. She won't want you to see any of this, and has to prepare in private, which takes the spontaneity away from any sexual encounter.

The other problem with period sex is the mess. Girls don't always find it a problem—they are familiar with the sight of blood and the mess it can make—but many men get squeamish. So, it's up to the both of you to decide what you want to do during this time of the month.

Effects of the Pill on Libido

The birth control pill is dangerous for the libido in a couple of ways. The lack of fluctuating hormones and chemical changes means a woman's sex drive can be leveled completely, keeping her libido even throughout her cycle. This is dangerous because if her libido is low, it could just stay that way. On the other hand, it could remain high. The pill does not often increase a woman's libido if it was previously low.

Birth control pills prevent ovulation, which is the peak of a woman's fertility, and therefore biological sexual desire. Her sex drive has to be carried through with other naturally made hormones (progesterone). This is not always a reliable bet, especially when artificial hormones are being pumped into the body.

In the search for better sex, let your awareness of the female species' clockwork menstrual cycle be your guide. Use it to your advantage and reap the benefits of both more sex and better sex, as well as enhanced communication with your partner. Knowledge is power!

8 SITUATIONS THAT MAKE WOMEN WANT SEX

Her libido obviously isn't dictated exclusively by her cycle; circumstances also have a bearing on how raring to go she'll be. So when you are practically guaranteed sex? Let's look at the 8 situations in which women are the horniest.

1. After an Argument

The concept of "make-up sex" is not a myth. A heated argument with your woman tends to get your blood boiling, and your heart pumping. And once you've both gotten whatever's been bothering you off your chests and told each other exactly how you feel, there's nothing quite like turning the tables by taking her in your arms, kissing her passionately, and letting your heightened emotions take over.

Even if you've upset her and she's crying, that's okay. Let her calm down, wipe her tears away, and make love to her.

2. Happy Occasion

Just like anger and sadness, extreme happiness can also get a woman in the mood. So, if she just got her degree, got a great new job, just found out she's pregnant, or another similarly joyous event has just taken place, it's time to channel all of that positive energy into some great sex.

3. Amid Stress

Stress isn't generally considered to be an extreme emotion, but it can raise a woman's libido. If your woman's been likened to a chicken without a head lately, chances are that she'd be quite appreciative if you offered her a release for her tension. That goes for stress-induced headaches too, by the way. That's right; a roll in the hay often gets rid of her headaches altogether. Be sure to tell her that the next time she gives you that tired line.

4. Jealousy

We're not talking jealousy of the psychotic kind here; we're referring to that little twinge of insecurity that comes over her when another woman is doing her competitive bitch thing and putting the moves on you, so to speak. After an evening of watching her man be hit on by other women, she may just want to remind you about one of the important reasons you're with her and not them. But don't go out of your way to make her jealous, that will just hurt and confuse her in the long run, diminishing the likelihood of your getting laid even further.

5. Party On

We're not advocating getting her drunk and taking advantage of her here. But, there's nothing like a little dancing and drinking to get a woman in the mood. So, pour her her favorite kind of liquid courage, lead her in a slow dance on your living room floor, and watch as her inhibitions slowly melt away, allowing you to proceed with the matter at hand.

6. Sexy Movie

A steamy sex scene starring her favorite Hollywood heartthrob may just be enough to get her revved up and ready for you. Turn your next hum-drum night in watching movies into a night you won't soon forget.

7. Abstinence

If the woman you're after has been single for a while, and isn't the one-night stand type, chances are that she's looking for the right guy to break her dry spell. It just may be you.

8. Creative Pitch

If your woman enjoys using her creativity, whether it be in the kitchen, with a paintbrush, or musically, these occasions may be conducive to great sex. So, the next time she's making you a gourmet meal, you may just want to slip into the kitchen for some pre-dinner sex.

Women want it more often than you may think. You just have to know how to recognize the moment, and seize it. So the next time she comes home stressed out from her day at work, instead of sulking that you won't be getting any that night, have a glass of wine while waiting for her, play some smooth tunes on the stereo, and offer to ease her mind. The ball's in your court.

FEMALE LIBIDO KILLERS

Here is a collection of sneaky things—from birth control to her level of activity—that may be affecting her sex drive.

Confidence

Confidence issues and stress are both major hindrances to a healthy sex life. Bad self-image is the worst offender, with weight issues topping the list. It can take a long time for a woman to get comfortable in her own skin, and the best thing you can do is reassure her that she is beautiful and desirable.

Anxiety

Anxiety relief is in order here, but how that is achieved is up to you and her. Take the bull by the horns, and provide a relaxing massage and a bit of pampering—this will go a long way.

Lack of Physical Exercise

Women who exercise regularly have higher sex drives and, more often than not, their periods are less painful and PMS is a lot less severe or even non-existent.

It can be an extremely stupid thing to suggest to a woman that she exercise more, so by suggesting physical things you can do together (like going for jogs or rollerblading), you are improving your own sex life (and overall health and happiness).

Toxic Overload

If we don't help our bodies clear out toxins, they will build up and give us zits, odors, and low energy levels. Smoking, pollution, lack of exercise, bad diet, and being overweight all make us feel less stellar than we should, and these factors also kill our sex drives.

The Birth Control Pill

As discussed earlier, the pill is dangerous for a woman's libido. Her hormones are leveled completely, which rules out the sexual peak at ovulation and just before her period. Going off the pill may not be the best idea, so get her to ask her doctor for an alternative type of birth control.

Antidepressants

Some antidepressants can increase libido in women, while others reduce it significantly. There are some that have had fewer reported sexual side effects, so if one antidepressant doesn't work well, there are other options.

---

4 REASONS WHY SHE STOPPED HAVING SEX WITH YOU

For every situation in which a woman does want to have sex, it seems that there's two in which she doesn't. Sometimes her absent libido can be ascribed to physical or environmental circumstances, but oftentimes her lack of enthusiasm is attributable to altogether different reasons—reasons which you may have a hand in. Read on to discover some of the major reasons why women stop having sex with their significant others and see why this stands true.

1. She's Angry at You

Most women cannot be intimate with a man that they're angry at. And unfortunately for you, many women bottle up their resentment, instead of simply letting you know when you've upset them. This means that your woman might be stark raving mad at you, even though you haven't the slightest clue that you've done anything wrong.

Solution: Talk to her and calmly ask her if you've done anything that has upset her lately. If she quickly says "no," and tries to change the subject, ask her again and encourage her to be honest with you. It's possible that after she gets what's bothering her off her chest, you two can have a mind-blowing round of make-up sex.

2. She's Overwhelmed

Maybe your woman isn't interested in sex because she is just overwhelmed with obligations lately. Between her work, workouts, night classes, family dinners, drinks with friends, cleaning the apartment, and cooking you dinner, it's a miracle that her head hasn't spun off.

Solution: When she gets home tonight, offer to help ease her load by cooking her dinner and doing the dishes. And tell her that she isn't allowed to do anything but sip a glass of wine and relax. She'll feel so loved and appreciated that she'll want to do anything to please you in return.

3. She Feels Unsexy

It's very simple: if your girlfriend feels unsexy, she won't want to have sex. Maybe she's put on a few pounds, she's exhausted, or someone insulted her. It's not uncommon for a woman to judge herself too harshly.

Solution: Encourage her to take some time to pamper herself. You could treat her to an afternoon at the spa, or, better yet, give her a long massage. Sometimes something as simple as paying her a genuine compliment will remind her how attractive you think she is, and get her raring to go.

4. She Thinks the Sex Is Boring

Perhaps the reason she no longer wants to have sex with you is because it has become a tad too dull and routine for her liking. If you catch her yawning amid sex, or worse, you'd rather be watching TV than pumping away, then chances are this the case.

Solution: Have sex in a different location, such as in a secluded outdoor spot. Incorporate aphrodisiacs, such as chocolate and strawberries, into your lovemaking. Buy her a naughty negligee or toy. You get the idea.

While there may be other reasons for her refusal to have sex with you, these are the most common. Some are easier to remedy than others. Sometimes all it takes is a little open communication.

HOW TO OVERCOME A WOMAN'S FEAR OF INTIMACY

You've probably encountered a woman with a fear of intimacy at some point in your life. She may have been outgoing and confident, shy and troubled, or a little bit of both. Whatever the case, she wasn't going to let just anyone get too close.

The problem was that you wanted to be close to her and, frankly, you didn't have a clue how to go about it. Here are a few ways to spot women who may suffer from a fear of intimacy, different causes of this fear, and, when possible, ways you can overcome it.

Poor Body Image

Every woman has an issue with some part of her body, such as her butt, thighs, or breasts. But there are two types of women: the ones that do something about it, such as exercise, eat properly, and take care of themselves; and the ones that feel victimized by their own bodies, and do nothing but complain about them. While the former are quite confident about the way they look, the latter's whole sense of self can be thrown off by something as seemingly insignificant as an advertisement.

This type of woman will often have a fear of intimacy, as she may think that men will judge her imperfect body as harshly as she does.

Overcoming this complex is difficult; feeling good in your own skin is pretty much a prerequisite for being able to have a mutually fulfilling relationship with another person. However, there are certain things you can do to make her feel more comfortable.

If she is self-conscious about her wide hips, and you happen to think they're sexy, tell her so often. Don't be afraid to grab them and caress them. Eventually, she'll forget why she had an issue with them and will let you get a closer look.

If her insecurity goes beyond this, try buying her a sexy nightgown, and ask her to put it on while you dim the lights. This way, she'll feel less self-conscious, and you'll score major points for being such a gentleman.

Inexperienced

Her fear of intimacy could also stem from a certain lack of experience. Maybe she is a virgin (yes, they do still exist), or maybe she has only had a couple of short-lived relationships. Or maybe her brand of inexperience is not so much sexual; perhaps it has more to do with the fact that she's been with the same person for years and the thought of being with someone completely new, while exciting, scares her.

Whatever the case, the key is to move very slowly and gain her trust by letting her know what a great guy you really are. Once you have that, you are free to make your first move. Remember to be gentle and guide her to the best of your abilities; she'll open up eventually.

Broken Heart

A woman may be hesitant to give her heart away if it has recently been broken. Maybe her last boyfriend didn't treat her properly or cheated on her. This case is tough because such a woman is in self-protect mode and only an incredible guy will be able to snap her out of it. In fact, this woman will only get into a new relationship if she feels that the guy in question is trustworthy and not out to hurt her.

The problem is that if you try to project such a persona in a forced manner, she'll pick you off as a phony, trying too hard, and your efforts will backfire. If you're sure that you really want to deal with this, you may want to encourage her to talk about her past with you, assuming that she even wants to. In this case, it's entirely up to her to decide when and with whom she will feel comfortable starting a new, hopefully very sexual, relationship.

Seen It All

Maybe the woman you're after is afraid because she's seen way too much for any one person to bear—too many dysfunctional relationships, seriously messed-up individuals, and enough hatred, greed, pain, jealousy, injustice, and misery to last a lifetime. Someone who knows just how ugly the dark side of human behavior can get will be very guarded as to whom they let into their lives.

Such a woman will generally have a certain intuition about people and will use it to her advantage to help determine who merits her trust. If she herself is kind-hearted, she will just want to know that you are, too, and that you are not prone to the various types of madness that she's seen in other people and situations. So, while you can still be mysterious, don't be mean.

A Matter of Trust

For women with a fear of intimacy, trust seems to be the order of the day. So if you aren't trustworthy, you're barking up the wrong tree. If, on the other hand, you can be trusted, then remember not to try to get into her head. While, deep down, everyone wants to be understood, no one wants to be psychoanalyzed by their lover—be a friend, not a therapist.

One last point: Don't misinterpret her lack of interest in you for a fear of intimacy; she may just not like you in that way. She might just be extremely choosy, and be holding out for the guy who she feels best meets her expectations.

6 KINKY THINGS SHE LOVES BUT WON'T TELL YOU

Here are six kinky things your gal might be fantasizing about, but is probably too shy to tell you.

1. Stroke It

Masturbation is a healthy part of life, so why not share it with your partner? If you're not too shy, put your guard down and let her watch as you get acquainted with yourself. The whole voyeurism element has a certain mystique that might appeal to her.

2. Fender Bender

Anal sex is an age-old activity, but it tends to have a negative stigma attached to it. This might be why some couples have yet to venture into this unknown territory, and why some women might be a little shy to suggest it. You can start slowly by spooning—this is a very slow and intimate way of initiating anal sex.

3. Tough Love

Is she a control freak? Then maybe she'd like to try a little S&M. It might get a little painful at times, so before the hot wax and nipple-pinching begins, make sure you've established a "safe word," like "zebra" or "mac and cheese," so she knows when to stop the torture.

4. Gadgets and Gizmos

Sex toys are a fun and exciting way to put some heat back in the bedroom. You can take baby steps and begin with heated and flavored massage oils, then try applying some orgasm-enhancing lubricant to her genitalia, and see how she likes it when you use a sex toy on her.

5. Curtain Call

Role-playing might be on her list of "must try" kinky fantasies. Map out interesting scenarios or pick real-life sexy couples to model yourselves after, then grab some fun costumes and let your imaginations guide you.

6. Three's a Crowd

That's right—having a threesome isn't just your fantasy. Some women have also entertained the idea. Something important to note—before you start running a list of her friends through your head as possible candidates—is that threesomes can be dangerous for a relationship. So, make sure you discuss it thoroughly beforehand and that you both understand what the boundaries and limits of this romp are.

POSITIONS FOR DIFFERENT BODY TYPES

Adapting to her often involves more than accommodating her character or personality type; it can also entail bringing your physiques into alignment with one another. Your physical shape, your height and your flexibility are all factors that you may think limit your sexual antics. Here's a quickie cheat sheet of sexual positions for good sex that take into account these important considerations.

Weight

There may be some embarrassment over those extra pounds, which can lead to a decreased sexual performance and over-sensitivity when paranoia and judgment rear their ugly heads. So, why not engage in some vigorous sexual activity to shed some calories? The more oxygen you burn, the more calories fly off. Sigh and moan your calories away with these groan-worthy moves.

Mechanical Drawing: If both partners are overweight, try this: Have the woman lie flat on her back and spread her thighs. The man can lie with his hips under her arched thighs. This allows your tummies room to breathe, yet connects you fully by your happy bits.

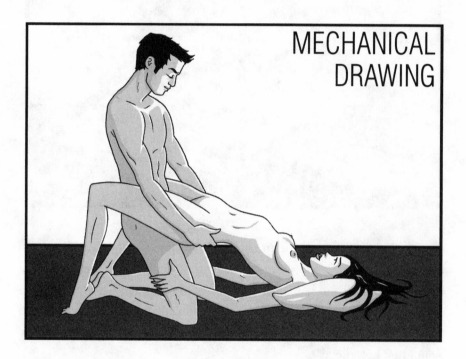

MECHANICAL
DRAWING

BAMBOO SPLIT

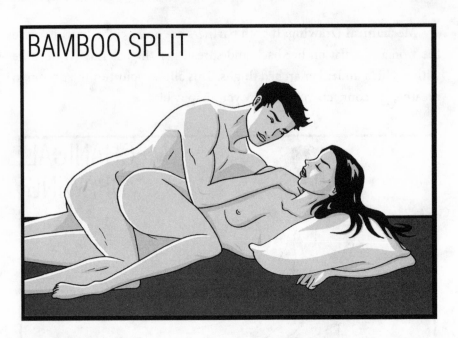

Bamboo Split: For the man who is of a normal weight and the woman who is deliciously voluptuous: Have your woman lie on her side then bring her upper leg to her chest, or as far as she can get it. Slide into position behind her and enter her from the rear and slightly to the side with your knees on each side of her bottom leg. You can control your thrusting by holding her upper leg.

A VIEW FROM BEHIND

A View from Behind: This position can be used with one or both partners being overweight. Standing and bent over, it's doggy style! Everyone knows this move. The important thing to remember is to have all your parts aligned and in the desired area. The man can lift his tummy to rest on her derriere to allow full penetration without undue interference from his stomach. You can both stand and have her rest her arms over a bed or a couch, depending on its height, or you can stand and deliver her a raging good time as she half lies on the edge of the bed with her knees drawn up and spread. You can also go down and surprise her with a passionate kiss on those pouty lips.

Height

Whether the man stands head and shoulders above her, or he buries his head in her breasts, the height differential carries the potential for challenge.

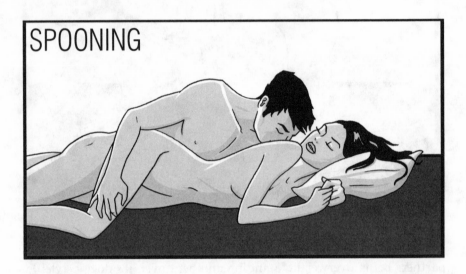

SPOONING

Spooning: A great position for lovers is the side-by-side spooning technique. It's intimate and loving. Height doesn't matter—either partner can be tall or vertically challenged. Just come up behind her and enter from behind. This kind of shallow thrusting calls for kissing her back, and caressing her nipples and clitoris with your free hands. For deeper penetration, you can both lie at opposing 45-degree angles where the apex is your blissful connection (looks like a V).

REVERSE COWGIRL

Reverse Cowgirl: This gives full and deep penetration. Have your girl straddle you facing your toes and enjoy watching her beautiful bum swallow you whole. Height differences will be out of mind as you enjoy the view.

KISS-OFF

The Kiss-Off: Miss the eye contact? The kissing? The full-body contact? Here's a position that will place vertically opposite bodies at nearly eye level. Sit up or recline slightly. Have her straddle you as you bounce her up and down, rock her sweetly and kiss her fervently. Your hands are free to roam as they please.

Flexibility

Have both you and your partner been blessed with extraordinary flexibility? If so, you're a lucky pair. Exploit your natural gifts with these positions, unavailable to most of the rest of the population.

MAN SQUAT

Man Squat: The woman should be fairly flexible as she lies on her back and arches her back like a U shape into the bed. The man is on his knees, back semi-bent, as he enters her and places her legs as far up his chest as they'll go. Some women can rest their knees on his shoulders, leaving a very steep and deep angle of penetration. Experiment to see what she's comfortable with.

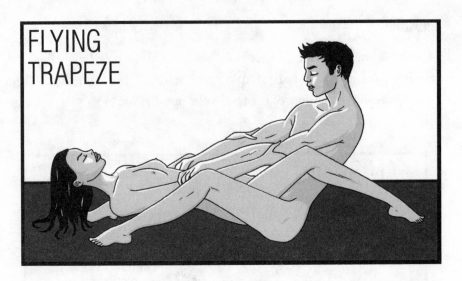

FLYING
TRAPEZE

Flying Trapeze: The man is sitting upright, legs stretched out like a V and slightly bent, while the woman lowers herself onto him, her legs bent over his. Grasping her wrists, the man holds her steady as she relaxes backwards nearly touching the ground. Rhythmically pull her toward you to get the thrusting sensation.

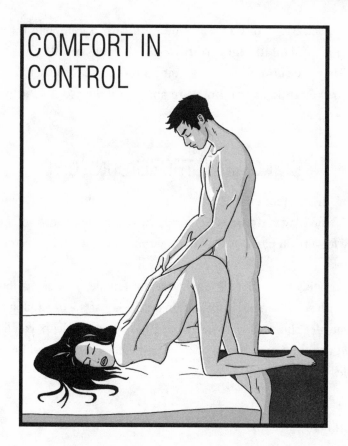

COMFORT IN
CONTROL

Comfort in Control: If you like to have control and your lover likes some mild domination, take her from behind with a twist. Position her on the edge of the bed. Place her on her knees and push her down so that her face is in the sheets and her behind is sticking up. Enter her slowly and draw her arms back. Instruct her to grasp your wrists/forearms as you hold hers tightly. Instigate your own engaging rhythm and/or aggressively deep penetration.

Cautionary note: Only go as far as she is comfortable. Don't try to force her legs/arms back, up, around, or bend her backwards further than she would normally go. If you see a strained look on her face and you know it isn't one of her "I need you now . . . I'm almost there" looks, you need to back off and proceed more gently.

These selections of moves are by no means a complete resource to pleasing a woman and man with weight, height, and flexibility differences. They are simply a starting point. Enjoying each other and fulfilling desires as fully as you both are able is the key to a healthy sexual relationship.

GOING AFTER THE REBOUND GIRL

Women on the rebound usually want sex with no strings—or so they think. If you play your cards right, you can reap the rewards of a woman hungry for a fresh partner. Play them wrong though, and you could be in for a mess.

Even if it's your first time playing the female "course" in question, armed with some general information on the lay of the psychological land and strategies about when to drive hard and when to lay up, you'll be able to avoid the emotional rough or the "player label" traps, and hit nothing but holes in one.

Rebound Girl

She either got dumped or left her boyfriend. If she seems bright enough about it, then either way, you win. All you have to do is seem better than him and you'll come up smelling like roses.

If she's on the prowl, then it's really a race to get her attention, as the first guy to make a move can get lucky—without setting himself up for a long-term relationship.

Remember: this is definitely not just about sex for her. She's looking for rebound sex because she wants to prove she's desirable. She wants to be sure that she did the right thing in leaving her guy if that's the way it went down. Or if she got dumped, she wants to believe that he was the one with issues.

All you have to do is press some of her psychological buttons (compliments) and stroke some of her physical ones, and it will be good times all around.

PROS OF PLAYING

Here are just a few reasons to bounce around with the newly available girl in town:

Easy sex: 'Nuff said.

Wild sex: She's got a lot of pent-up energy and is looking to be reminded of what else sex can be like.

She wants freedom (i.e., no strings): If she was dumped, she wants to feel in control. Hey, being on the bottom ain't so bad. Or maybe she wants a guy to take more control than the last guy did.

CONS OF PLAYING

Knowing what to expect is the best way to be prepared so that you can avoid unpleasant surprises. Here are just a few of the cons of hanging with a rebound girl.

She has emotional baggage: This is where it gets tricky. For a woman, rebound sex is like a one-night girls-only trip to Club Med—an escape. So keep conversations light and avoid any deep emotional topics. Being her friend and offering her a shoulder to cry on is the last thing you want to do.

She's likely to suck up to get what she wants—sex: This can falsely prop up your ego and cause you to get attached. Remember: people on the rebound need space and an escape. Bear all this in mind and take it all in stride, and you run less risk of getting your own ego bruised.

Easy come, easy go: Be prepared for the unexpected. She's having fun and doesn't really care if she hurts you. After all, she's been hurt, and you can bet that she might be trying to do her fair share of heart-breaking. So when she stops calling, take it as a sign that it's over and don't chase her.

Her boyfriend comes back: Women who get dumped have a high rate of return. If it happens to you, don't sweat it. Just give the poor old fellow a few bedroom tips about what his girlfriend likes. Don't forget to smile.

Let's say you're in a bar or at a party with a couple of friends, and you successfully glom onto a group of attractive ladies. You are moving in on the hottest one, who, as is often the case, is not the most interesting or outgoing.

After a few jokes, you pay her a killer compliment, she blushes, and you ask whether it's a girls' night out, and if that's why she's left her boyfriend behind for the evening.

"Actually, I just got out of something pretty serious," she says.

"Oh," you say, sounding neither surprised nor lewd, but neutral.

The Approach

Now just because she doesn't seem like the life of this party, it doesn't mean she wouldn't like to come alive in a more private venue. But you must pay very close attention to this initial disclosure, noting her facial expression and body language, because she's not telling you this just to make conversation.

It means one of two things:

1. It's a warning sign—"treat me gently, I'm fragile right now" kind of thing;

2. It's an invitation.

If she brings it up in a happy or "down with relationships, it's time to party" tone, make some kind of clear move (significant casual touching such as a squeeze on the shoulder) immediately, so she knows it's on.

Say something like: "Hey, maybe now's the perfect time to enjoy the single life. I'm headed down to an after-hours party later on. How would you and your lady friends like to come along?"

If you're not getting any buying signals here, it's time to move onto the next course.

Here are some tips for the go-ahead:

Move Quickly

If she doesn't do anything with you, it will probably be the next guy. Keep in mind that she could go back to her ex, so you need to show her that tonight, you're the hottest ticket she's going to come across.

Listen to Her

Say things like "I can't believe your ex did that to you." Be sensitive, but don't probe for too much info. Segue to a related but lighter topic as soon as sensitivity permits and you won't get caught in any emotional crevasses or be labeled "the friend."

Read Her

Get a feel for her to see if she's reserved or wild. Then mirror her. If wild, welcome her rebellious behavior both verbally and physically.

Compliment Her

Remember the ego stroking? First, mention something slightly negative (the famous negative hit) to position yourself as a bit of a challenge, then turn it into a joke/compliment.

Have Fun

Don't pressure her. And, as always, be detached from the situation enough to show that you're enthusiastic, but in the end you could take it or leave it.

Don't Show Too Much Emotion

She's got enough of her own, and either resents or is sick of her ex-boyfriend's. Be a rock up front and she'll want to get her rock on.

Keep Your Mouth Shut

In other words, don't divulge too much information about yourself and remain a mystery.

The Final Tally

Heading straight for the hole on someone in such a potentially vulnerable situation could seem callous. But if she's welcoming your respectable advances, you gauge she's up for a good time, and you're both keeping the whole rebound tryst factor in perspective, why would two consenting adults turn down such a plum situation?

PROS AND CONS OF DATING AN OLDER WOMAN

Think of how much your attitude regarding sex has changed over the years. Men's approaches toward and reactions to women evolve drastically over the years, and guess what? Theirs do, too. So it's no surprise that we have to craft our approach differently to women of different age. Let's have a look at the art of picking up older women.

The Cons

Bag lady

Common sense dictates that you cannot be 40 years old and single, and not have some baggage. Ex-boyfriends, husbands, children, ex-step-children, pending divorces, business pressures, financial obligations, and debts can often be part of the package.

You must be ready and willing to accept this reality if you are going to get romantically linked with an older woman. Realize that an older woman generally has more to worry about than that bushy-tailed coed at your dorm.

Mrs. Robinson

One cannot deny the allure of the older woman–younger man relationship. But, this relationship remains slightly taboo, unlike its commonly accepted reverse, in which the man is much older than the woman.

Like it or not, by getting involved with an older woman, you put yourself in a situation in which the moral majority—people like your parents and your boss—will frown upon you. On the up side, you may become your buddies' hero, and they may beg you to reveal what it's like.

In any case, people will talk. If you are secure enough in the relationship, or you actually like the attention, then, by all means, proceed.

The cougar

A breed of older women have been dubbed "cougars" for a reason: They hunt younger men.

In this type of relationship, the woman is often in control. Some think that a woman who dates a younger man does so because she can easily manipulate him; that the man in question will be so awestruck by her attention that he will go along with whatever she says. But that is a theory that does not necessarily apply to every situation.

The Pros

Boy toy

Often, available older women are newly divorced, and looking to sow their wild oats. Getting involved with a man who isn't looking for a serious relationship and wants to have fun is the perfect solution.

Younger men have the stamina and carefree attitude to satisfy their need for a wild ride. So, if you're looking to learn a thing or two between the sheets, look no further than an older woman. After all, she's no longer sexually inhibited, knows what she wants, and probably has a few tricks up her sleeve.

She's over it

More often than not, an older woman has faced her insecurities and fears head on, and has dealt with them to the best of her abilities. She likely has enough life experience to know what matters and what doesn't. Consequently, she's above the petty nonsense that drives you crazy about women your own age. An older woman has figured out what makes her look fat and what looks good on her, and knows enough about male-female relationships to not bother you with feminine trivialities that usually serve to turn men off anyway.

Older women have the self-confidence that comes from experience and the knowledge that they can handle whatever life throws their way. That is not to say that they never have a bad day, but that if they do, it's probably due to something more than the fact that they have a pimple and a party to go to that night.

Go for It

In the end, it's up to you to weigh the pros and cons of such a relationship and decide if it is right for you right now. Let's see, the promise of mind-blowing sex with an experienced, confident woman, without the expectation of a long-term commitment . . . it's a tough call.

RULE 10: EXPRESS YOURSELF

Remember Rule 2, Conversation? Well, the importance of communication doesn't fade after the pickup. It's fundamental in any relationship, whether serious or casual, both to reinforce the good elements, and to redirect the negative ones. And nowhere is this more important than in the sack. It's important to talk about what you like, and things you'd like to change about your relationship. Mastering the art of talking dirty doesn't hurt, either.

DISCUSS WHAT YOU WANT IN BED

Most couples fear that mentioning something that they don't like will turn into an argument. That doesn't have to be the case. Life is only as complicated as you make it and if you want her to do something you like, or stop doing something you hate, then you have to let her know. No one likes to be criticized, to say the least, but there are ways to get your point across without causing emotional damage.

Play for Directions

One of the best ways you can get to know what she likes when it comes to making love is to play the directions game. All you have to do is tell each other what to do.

When she makes her way down to your penis, direct her on what to do. Say things like, "go as low as you like . . . slowly . . . come back up . . . kiss the head . . . use your hand to stroke my penis . . . rub my anus . . ." I think you get the gist of it. But keep in mind that this shouldn't be robotic talk. Whisper, moan with pleasure when she gets it right, and when you get really excited, let her hear it.

She can tell you what to do; she can hold onto your hair and swing her hips while you keep your tongue in the same place for her to maneuver until it hits the perfect spot. Make it fun; laugh together.

We Need to Talk

If she bites your penis all the time and thinks you like it, or if you know that she's been faking her way through sex to get it over with, then maybe it's time the two of you talked about sex openly and honestly.

But rather than tell her all the things she does wrong, maybe you should focus instead on reinforcing what she does right and what you'd like her to do to you. Remember that when you say something negative like, "I hate it when you . . ." you're asking for an argument because you're broaching it the wrong way.

Say things like, "I love it when you . . ." and "I want you to lick my [insert body part here] because I know that your tongue will work wonders on it." Be creative and it will never be taken as criticism.

Without Saying a Word

The two of you can also get naked and sit in front of each other. Take your time with each other and glide your hands along her body.

Slowly, and with patience, begin kissing and caressing areas that you usually end up skipping over amid foreplay and sex. Spend time smelling her neck, run your fingers down her spine, nibble on her hips and thighs; do the things that will turn her body and mind on.

When you've explored her areas thoroughly, let her do the same to you. Slowly, she'll find spots that will make you crazy. You might even end up discovering new things about your own body and what turns you on.

Take Your Time

When it comes to having sex, there's never a need to rush (unless you have to be at work in 15 minutes), so don't hurry things along and don't skip the foreplay because that's what leads up to incredible sex.

If you're able to engage in sex with your partner, you should definitely be able to discuss your likes and dislikes with her.

Or better yet, instead of having sex with each other right away, take the time to get to know each other and, through some hot conversations, figure out what she likes and let her figure out what gets you going.

The Bottom Line

If you never tell her what you like, she may never find out. And if you want to please her, then accept some of the constructive criticism that she may hand out. Keep in mind, however, that she may not know how to be tactful when discussing sex.

If you're at a point in your relationship where you're comfortable with each other, then it's okay to be perfectly honest with her—after all, if you're not happy with the quality of your sex life, then other areas of your relationship may begin to suffer.

You're not trying to start a fight; you want to understand her and have her understand you so that you can add a twist to what could potentially be the greatest sex you'll ever have.

GIVE HER FEEDBACK ABOUT SEX

Wouldn't it be great if you could tell your woman anything you wanted without repercussion? Well, that's never going to happen. But there are ways to criticize what she does in bed—without hurting her feelings—that will encourage her to please you.

Here are the most common complaints guys have about their women, and how they should address the issues:

Instead of Saying: "You Should Make the First Move Sometimes."

First, reveal a fantasy in which she initiates the sex. Discuss in detail how she seduces you.

If that doesn't do it, say something like, "It must bother you that I'm always coming on to you . . . actually, I'd be so turned on if you came on to me." And if and when she does, always react positively.

Instead of Saying: "You're Awful at Giving Oral Sex."

First, reveal the things you *do* like about what she does when she goes down on you.

Next, consider renting porn. There's nothing like a good role model to steer 'em right.

Finally, direct her gently. When she's doing something right, moan and let her know with reassuring words.

Instead of Saying: "Man, Your Vagina Stinks!"

Don't say anything. Instead, take her into the shower before sex and clean her up. Let her do the same for you, otherwise she might suspect something.

Then, smell her all over and tell her how much you appreciate this fresh scent of hers. And of course, when you give her oral sex, let her know that you enjoy the taste of her *fresh* lips.

Instead of Saying: "I Hate It When You . . ."

Start off by engaging in role-play. But don't play doctor or pimp. Instead, assume her role in the bedroom and let her assume yours. This way, you can *show* her what you want her to do. Showing her how good something feels will steer her in the right direction.

And if that doesn't work, tell her that you don't enjoy it when she sucks your nipples, for instance, because they're too sensitive. Do your best not to sound negative (avoid words like never, don't, hate, and no) but get your message across nevertheless.

Don't Be Blunt

Some women think that all guys like the same thing in bed. It's up to you to make it clear that that's not true. Without sounding harsh and insulting her, let her know what you want in bed and what you don't want.

THE BEST THINGS TO SAY TO WOMEN IN BED

Women are verbal creatures at heart. That's why they read erotica, get hooked on soaps, and love men with foreign accents. These things make them feel the same way we do when we spot a beautiful woman with huge breasts.

Though what excites them is drastically different from what arouses us, there's good news there. If you can paint a picture with a few choice words, you can turn them on. So it's in our best interests to learn to say the right things. With that in mind, here are the best things to say to a lady once you separate her from those pesky clothes.

"I Want to Make You Feel Good."

Simple, yet effective. A wonderful way to relax her and reassure her that she made the right decision going to bed with you. Drop this one right before or during foreplay for maximum effect.

"I Love the Sounds You Make When You Orgasm."

If you know your girl well and know that she does, indeed, orgasm, then this one is for you. And sometimes, even if she does orgasm, a woman feels awkward being vocal during sex. But most of us like a loud woman in bed, because it helps us to know when you're pleasing her. So you can encourage her to turn up the volume by telling her how much you enjoy it.

"You Have Such (a) Hot [insert body part]."

Pick a favorite body part to mention, but make it one you know she's proud of. That way, there's no controversy. Women are notorious for being sensitive to clumsy compliments about their bodies, so tread carefully.

"I Love the Way You Taste. I Could Stay Down Here for Hours."

This reassures her that you like giving her oral sex and that there are no foul odors emanating from that area. You can say this one during a short break from oral sex or directly afterwards.

"What Are You Imagining Right Now?"

This will encourage her to talk about her sexual desires and participate in setting the mood. The idea here is to let her release any bottled-up fantasies or requests that she would otherwise not mention.

"This Feels So Good. I Love It When You [insert action here]."

Again, this is meant to boost her comfort level (and ego) with a little positive feedback. And, hey, if she knows you like something, perhaps she'll take note for future reference.

"You're So Good at [insert action here]."

Let her know when she's doing something you like. Like us, women take special pride in being good in bed. This phrase is best said with an air of disbelief and an emphasis on "so."

"Your Skin Is So Soft and Smooth."

Ladies spend a lot of time rubbing things such as cocoa butter on their bodies after a shower. It's time we appreciated this strange ritual with a well-placed compliment. Because this is a seductive remark, it's best to say it *before* sex. However this could also double for use during pillow talk.

"I Want to Kiss Every Inch of You."

Women love foreplay and they love to be pampered. Even if you don't actually intend on kissing every inch of her body, she'll know your heart is in the right place. What you're telling her is that you love and appreciate all of her. It's very comforting to hear.

"I've Never Felt This Good Before."

Women love to be singled out as special, different, and unique. If she does something to you in bed that has never been done so pleasurably before, tell her as much. Say it so sincerely that she thinks you're going to name your car after her. Just don't trip up and say something like "It's the best ever," which would be overdoing it.

"You're So (expletive) Hot!"

Straightforward is often the best way to go. And swearing is one way to tell her that you really mean it. Women often respect the take-charge John Wayne routine.

Be sure to gauge how she reacts to what you say. If you've been dating for months and suddenly break out the dirty talk in bed, she might be a little taken aback by your potty mouth.

Choose Your Words Wisely

It shouldn't come as a shock that women love men who say all the right things. It's the second best way they like us to use our tongues. So study the phrases above and adapt them to your own ends.

TALKING DIRTY IN BED

Just the other night, while you and your girlfriend were in bed getting it on, she managed to get her lips close enough to your ear and whispered those four little words that leave just about every man completely confused: "Talk dirty to me."

So now what do you say? What does she want to hear exactly? Is she expecting porno talk or does she want you to be suave and use creative language to describe her genitalia? There's only one way to find out . . .

Study Your Woman

You have to watch and listen to how she behaves. Could she give sailors a run for their money with her vulgar language? Or is she more laid-back, preferring the use of million-dollar words to communicate what she's thinking?

Of course, this hint alone determines nothing. Many women act sweet and innocent in public, but become savage beasts and use the most colorful language ever heard in the bedroom. And then there are the "tough girl" beauties, who put on an independent façade but became quiet little bunnies in the bedroom.

Next, how does she like her lovemaking? Does she like to take things slowly and quietly, or is she more of a wild woman who likes to experiment with light bondage and the outdoors?

Again, these clues may not set her dirty talk request in stone, but chances are you can delve into the more raunchy language when engaging in raunchier sex.

Test the Dirty Waters

Of course, you needn't wait on her to initiate the dirty talk—there's nothing to stop you from doing so. The first step in introducing this element into lovemaking is to test the waters in casual conversation. Ask questions like: "Have you ever talked dirty in bed before?" or "If I talked filth into your ear while we made love, what would you do?" This gets the idea into her head, and rest assured that she'll ponder it after you mention it, and possibly discuss it with her girlfriends to see what they do and if they like it.

It is possible, however, that she will flatly refuse to entertain the idea, in which case, it's best to drop it. If she is uncomfortable with the idea, she is not likely to change her mind in a hurry and any attempts will probably be a turn off.

There are two aspects of successfully integrating dirty talk into your sex play:

1. The content: Subject matter makes or breaks any dirty talk session. It's supposed to turn her on, not make her cringe or burst out laughing.

2. The delivery: Your tone, volume, and the warm-up are all important.

Before You Start

There are certain things you must keep in mind when it comes to dirty talk in order to maintain a happy relationship:

Leave it in the bedroom

Don't take what happens in the bedroom out in public. That means that you don't get to swear at her or make lewd requests when you're having dinner at a nice restaurant—unless, of course, she asks you to.

Don't disrespect her

Even when you do talk dirty, remember that you're living out a fantasy with her. So that doesn't mean that she really thinks she's a bitch or what have you. Rather, she simply enjoys being treated like a bad girl on occasion. Separate fantasy from reality.

Explain that it's playtime

Sometimes it's hard for your woman to distinguish if you're just playing around or actually mean the nasty things you're saying. Make sure she feels comfortable with your dirty talk by explaining that it's just a fantasy.

Start out slow

It's better to be safe than sorry so it's best to start out by saying tamer things and with tamer language (for instance, "I've been wanting to get inside you all day"), and slowly moving on to the cruder lingo in time.

Turn the tables on her

The best way to encourage dirty talk is by assuming a different role in the bedroom. You submit and let her be more dominant. This way you'll get more of a clue as to what she means when she mentions "dirty talk." You need directions and she's the only one who knows the route.

Delivering the Goods

1. Choose a voice

What is sexy to you? Low and deep, high and squeaky, or a breathy whisper? Your normal talking voice or a new persona? Play around with a few and choose one you like. The benefit of having a special dirty talk voice is that when you are on the phone with her in the future and you use your sexy voice, her mind will automatically associate that voice with (hopefully) raunchy, exciting sex.

2. Warm up

First thing's first: Make sure you are both in the mood. It is easiest to start talking dirty when you are actually having sex. You will both need to be quite turned on for it to work, which means no skipping foreplay. Whisper a couple of things in her ear and see what she does, just to test the waters.

3. Start talking

A good way to start the dirty talk is by simply relaying what you are doing at the time and how good it feels—but don't go on about it. Having someone commentating on the action the entire time can be a turn off, so take it easy. Just say a few things, like: "Your [insert body part] feels so good" or "I love how my [insert body part] feels when you do that." Keep in mind that women can feel quite self-conscious when a man comments on their body during sex. The benefit of this dialogue is that not only will she get to hear you dirty talk, but she'll also get to learn more about what you like during sex. This communication has longer-lasting benefits than just making sex more exciting at the time, and it will encourage her to speak up too.

4. Develop your repertoire

Try to keep the subject matter and the lines you use varied; nobody likes a broken record. Once you are more confident that she likes it and wants to play, try to incorporate some speech-centered role-playing into your lovemaking. Get her to join in; you may just find her swearing back at you.

5. Get feedback

It can be hard to discuss how well you're doing whilst in the act, so save the analysis for later. If she doesn't like it but you clearly do, she won't want to embarrass you. To avoid this problem with a less communicative partner, ask her later. Discuss it when you're watching TV or making dinner. Any time you are fully clothed there is a far less risk of damaging egos. You can talk about which parts you both liked, and if she or you stopped liking it at any time and why. Keep the discussion light-hearted and fun.

6. Prepare to deal with laughter

We laugh at all sorts of things, especially when we're nervous or afraid. The problem with talking dirty is that it can often be hilarious and laughing is involuntary, or your nerves or hers may manifest themselves into laughter. To avoid this, discuss your fears with your partner, or at least mention that you are afraid that she will laugh at you. This lets her know not to laugh, but to encourage you and tell you what she would like.

DIRTY TALK DOS & DON'TS

Do: Read Her an Erotic Story

There are plenty of good erotic writers around, but finding something she will like can be hard. A good bet is to find a women's magazine that has an erotic fiction section in it or—even better—a specialized erotica magazine.

Do: Swear

Dirty words are part of our culture, and we use them for effect and expression. This is the very reason why swearing is a great part of talking dirty in bed. The bare-bones filth of the words spurs on the rawness of the act you are performing.

Do: Speak in a Different Language

All in all, English is not the most romantic language on earth. It is by no means the worst sounding, but something like French, Italian, or Portuguese sounds so much better. It sounds *different* and the words, spoken with such elegance, are a pleasure to hear.

Don't: Mention Family

References to her family or yours are strictly out of bounds and, really, do you want to be discussing the in-laws while you make love? Probably not. Don't mention anything about her super-sexy younger sister, either, or she'll pull the plug on the whole lovemaking shebang.

Don't: Talk About Other Women

Don't bring up the topic of other women unless she *specifically* requests it, otherwise it could make her feel very insecure. And insecurity is not a known aphrodisiac.

Don't: Use Clinical or Childish Terms

Clinical terms will sweep the sexiness out of any passionate moment. Calling your manhood an erect penis kills the moment with images of high school sex ed.

Softcore Dirt

Although we all refer to bedroom talk as dirty talk amid sex, there are two levels to it: the soft and the hard. If your woman enjoys using different words to describe your penis besides the usual four-letter words we're accustomed to, then by all means, think of different ways to say what she wants to hear.

The following are only a couple of examples of what she may want to hear:

1. The thought of you wrapping your hot mouth around my pulsating rod drives me crazy.

2. I love when you spread your thighs for me; open up and let me devour your juices.

Of course, with time you will come up with many creative words to replace vagina, penis, fellatio, cunnilingus, and the like. And don't let her get away with "yes" and "no" replies either. Ask her what she wants from you, what she imagines you doing, and how she imagines you going about it. As well, some women might find this kind of talk sappy. So listen to the language she uses and if she gets graphic, then move on to . . .

Hardcore Dirt

In the complete throes of passion, many people have been known to yell out some of the kinkiest, if not nastiest, phrases known to man. So you can get nasty and fill in all of the following gaps with some of the most vulgar language you can think of.

If you want to scream and yell or get close to her ear and whisper it lightly, that's up to you. But for the sake of giving you ideas, here are a few things you could say in the heat of the moment (not for the faint of heart):

1. I want to [fill in verb] you with my hard [fill in noun] until you [fill in verb] all over me.

2. I want you to suck my [fill in noun] while I suck on your throbbing [fill in noun].

3. (Put her up against the wall and put your hand up her skirt.) Do you like it when I stick my finger inside your wet [fill in noun]? I've been waiting all day to bend you over and [fill in verb] you deep and hard.

Take Over, Buddy

It's time for you to take creative initiative and tell it like it is. Whether she likes it soft-core or hard, add some fun to your bedroom experience by giving her a speech she won't soon forget.

Keep in mind, however, that talking dirty is not necessary during every sexual session and sometimes silence can say so much. So take it easy and work your way into it.

INTRODUCE YOUR KINKY SIDE

So you like wearing a thong when you go to dinner? Or being tied up and spanked? Well, you're certainly not alone. The trouble is, in our oh-so-modern sexual era (not!) bringing up fetishes and kinky pastimes with your new lover may not go down too well. At best, she will grin seductively and reveal that she too loves to do those things. At worst, she will think you are a pervy-weirdo creep and be unsure if she should see you again. If the former happens, well that's great. The latter? Read on, friend. We don't want you or your new girl getting your pink frillies in a twist.

Women Like Kinky Sex

Even the most prudish woman can be convinced to partake in the most lascivious and lewd sex acts. Despite rumors, more often than not, women are actually deviant sex goddesses waiting to be released from their good-girl prisons. The main factor when introducing new games to the bedroom is preparation; there should be very few surprises. This means—oh yes, you guessed it—lots of talking . . . preferably before you leap into bed.

Timing is not everything, but rates highly. Educating her is paramount. Making it seem like her idea in the first place is simply genius . . . if you can pull it off.

Introducing Spanking, Biting, and Hair-pulling

These are such childish behaviors, but they can add an uninhibited edge to good sex. The good thing about these is that you don't really have to talk about them too much before you do them. You can test the waters as you go along, but always keep it light. There are very few preconceived ideas about spanking, biting, and hair pulling.

How to introduce it: These things are best done during a very passionate sexual encounter. Go with the flow and use your common sense— tread deliberately and carefully. Wild abandon usually equals pain.

Spanking: The problem with spanking is it gets better the more you do it, and the first couple can sting quite badly. Let her spank you back. Have a good spanking session, laugh your heads off and spank each other silly. The eroticism will come later. Don't spank every session unless requested.

Biting: The success of your nibbles relies heavily on pressure, timing, and frequency. Keep it light, only do it while in the absolute throes of passion, and don't do it often. If you want her to bite you, instruct her on the art—she is unlikely to just know how you like it. Don't ever bite breasts or vaginas unless expressly asked to. Leaving marks is not desirable.

Hair-pulling: If you want to pull her hair, do it gently. If you want her to pull yours, then just asking nicely should yield results. There are loads of pressure points in the scalp that makes hair pulling quite a sensuous activity when done properly. Don't yank, and be conscious that her head and neck is attached to that beautiful hair. Hold the hair close to the scalp and in handfuls as opposed to pulling on a ponytail or the ends of longer hair.

Introducing Sex Toys

Times are changing, and it is entirely acceptable for a man to declare his longings for sex toys to be introduced into the bedroom repertoire. It is great to have a man who isn't insecure about it. Just be careful when pulling out butt plugs or prostate massagers because she is unlikely to be familiar with these. A vibrating plastic vagina might be on the weird side, and she may not know how to use a cock ring, or have ever seen a French tickler before, but no doubt she will embrace them with enthusiasm once given a quick lesson. But what if she doesn't?

There is a small chance she might think you are weird, in which case, you simply need to educate her so she is no longer afraid of the strange objects you wish to bring into the bedroom. The first step is to talk about it, especially if the toy is not standard issue vibrating material.

How to introduce it: Bring up the topic of toys at an apt time in an appropriate tone—that tone being a lighthearted and playful one. Certain toys will require a thorough explanation, so take care to explain the purpose of each toy, how it works, and what she can expect. She doesn't want to feel like an uneducated sex toy klutz if she has never used one before.

Introducing Light Bondage

Yes, she has a view on this particular pastime, even if she has never ever done it. She might think it is fun and sexy, or she might think it is scary and weird. Just so you know, most women view this as sexy, not weird.

But whatever her view, make sure you know what it is. Talk with her. You must always have permission.

How to introduce it: Next time you're in the throes of passion, hold her wrists above her head or by her sides and tease her with your hands or mouth or a feather. Hold her wrists lightly so that when she tries to wriggle free, she can't move unless she pushes against you firmly. Tease her some more, and then whisper seductively in her ear: "Can I tie you up and tease you until you have an orgasm/can't stand it any longer/want me to stop?" Then, do your thing!

Some guidelines: One at a time: don't both be tied up on the same occasion. If you are using rope, hemp is soft and won't burn. Cotton is good because it's soft, but fraying may be a problem. Synthetic rope will probably give rope burn, so unless you enjoy the pain, give it a miss. Try pulling out some fluffy handcuffs or a scarf. Save the blindfold for another day. Keep some blunt-ended scissors handy and always check the temperature of tied-up body parts (hands, feet) to ensure that they aren't getting too cold—a sign that her circulation may be getting cut off. They need to be released. Never refuse to release someone unless this is part of your sex game. If this is the case, use safe words. Never tie anything around someone's neck.

Introducing Anal Sex

So you like it in reverse? Good for you. The problem is, she might be horrified by the idea. This makes your job extra hard: Not only do you have to remove all the old ideas, but you need to replace them with new, convincing ones.

How to introduce it: When you think you have a clue of how to do it properly, bring it up. A simple "Have you ever had anal sex and enjoyed it?" works. There are only two answers to this question. If the answer's "yes," ask if she would like to do it again. If the answer's "no," ask if she would be brave enough to try it with you. Pull out your instructions and educate her. Every woman can enjoy anal sex if it's done right.

The orgasms are different, and can be quite intense. Pull out your instructions. Sell it to her. And use lube.

What not to do: It is not cool to just try to put it in "by mistake." This is excruciatingly painful. Always have permission, and never pressure her. The trick is getting her to want it.

Coming Out About a Fetish

A fetish can be a strange thing to observe in somebody, and even stranger to observe in yourself. For those without a fetish, it is very hard to understand what it's like to be aroused by an inanimate object that normally isn't associated with sex. If you have a fetish, denying it is futile. It is a part of who you are. The best thing you can do is to make sure you are totally comfortable with it yourself before sharing it with the person you love, if indeed you choose to share it. Some people keep it to themselves their whole lives, and it seems a shame that something you love so much has to be hidden.

Fear of rejection is high on the list of reasons not to tell, but if you are in a loving and healthy relationship, surely sharing a part of yourself can only make it stronger? If you are worried about sharing a fetish, you are certainly not alone. Before taking the leap, find a fetish community and talk to others about it and see what they have done, haven't done, or wished they had done. Only you can decide if it is the right thing to do.

Kink It Up

Introducing your new lady friend to your preferred bedroom antics can be nerve racking. This is with good reason—she may not react well. Don't forget that you can get away with just about anything if you approach it in the right way: Discuss it, educate her, keep it light-hearted, and you may just get your wish. Women love to try new things and be kinky minxes, but it will take a little while for them to build up trust and confidence with a new man. The great thing about it is that you are the new man, and she is free to explore her sexuality. Use this newness to your advantage, but don't forget: Only fools rush in.

ROLE PLAYING FOR BEGINNERS

Sometimes, it's easier to express one's sexual desires after taking on a different persona. Role playing can be loads of fun, provided it is done with a pinch of panache and a slice of sophistication. Pretending you are somebody else allows you to venture places you wouldn't normally go. It means you are voluntarily forced to go outside your comfort zone, and into another—acting. The world is your oyster, so suck it up; it's not every day you get to take on a completely different persona.

Expectations can be thrown out the window, traditions flushed down the toilet. The time you spend role playing will be well spent communicating with and pleasuring yourself and your lover.

Learn about some basic scenarios to find one that will suit both your tastes.

Headmistress and Pupil

Description: This role play dabbles with the rich fantasy world of teenage boys, and quite possibly, the headmistress. The pupil is under the instruction and discipline of the headmistress. This creates a power imbalance, which can be fun to take advantage of with a lover. Delving into your inner teenager while your lover delves into her inner headmistress is a fun way for you to be dominated by her. It gives her power and control, leaving you at her mercy, though there is always the chance of rebellion.

Sample scenario 1: The scene is set in the headmistress's office, with the pupil in school uniform, and the headmistress dressed looking very stern and serious, but sophisticated and incredibly sexy. The pupil has always had a crush on the headmistress, and was spying on her through her door, masturbating. The headmistress caught him, and saw he was doing it the wrong way. She now teaches him, in the privacy of her office, how to masturbate correctly. If he does it wrong, spanking may be involved.

Sample scenario 2: The headmistress calls the pupil to her office after school for disciplinary action. The pupil must write down every sexual thought and fantasy he has. Then he must read them back to the headmistress, who gets very aroused at the suggestions, which often include her. She then gives the pupil a lesson he will never forget on how to satisfy a woman the correct way. If he gets it wrong, he may be spanked. Or he may be spanked anyway.

Props: Spanking instrument (e.g., plastic ruler), school uniform, pad and pen.

Boss and Secretary

Description: This scene revolves around the work situation, and the power exchange that frequently takes place between a woman and her male boss. It is supposed that the boss is in control and calls the shots, but when sex is involved, this shifts to a dangerously sexy level where the woman is actually calling the sexual shots. She loves this because it gives her the power in that particular situation, even if she has none (or very little) at other times at work.

Sample scenario 1: The secretary hides underneath the boss's big desk before an important meeting. The secretary slowly—and very quietly—performs oral sex on the boss while he is in the middle of an important business deal. The clients are sitting right in front of the desk. He has to keep a straight face and continue on with his meeting. Alternatively, he may be on the phone (doing this for real is fun) and has to continue with his phone conversation without faltering.

Sample scenario 2: On a more voyeuristic note, the secretary wears some very, very sexy underwear to work. She has to try to show her boss what she is wearing underneath in any way she can while still maintaining a "professional" appearance. She teases him as she does the photocopying, while she puts papers on his desk, while he is talking to her. She has to seduce him without taking her clothes off, until he is gagging for it. A strip tease can also be incorporated into this scenario, where he cannot touch her until she says so.

Props: Desk or table, office attire.

Stripper and Client

Description: This role play is focused on voyeurism, but also on lack of emotion in sex. A lap dance is a deeply sensual act, and when done properly, leaves both participants feeling rather randy.

Remember: Erotic dancing can be a tough call, especially if a woman is very conscious of her body. A great way to offset these fears is to use lighting, stockings, and makeup. Dim lights tone skin nicely, as do red lights (covering a normal lamp with red material also works). Any lumps and bumps are smoothed out. Keep in mind that the removal of all clothes is not strictly necessary, so let her know to feel free to keep on a sexy-but-supportive bra, or a lovely pair of knickers, or both. As long as the moves are hot and the lighting is appropriate, it will look beautiful and the effect will be the same.

If finding some moves is a problem, look up dancing videos on the web, or, if you dare, go into a real strip club and see what they do. Most cities around the globe now have strip workout classes available for women (and possibly men) which are a fantastic way to get fit and release the sensual beast inside.

Sample scenario 1: A dancer in a club is solicited to do a private dance. She takes him into her private booth and closes the curtains, then proceeds to give him the striptease of his life. There are rules: no touching and no kissing. He may put money down her garter belt. He must keep his clothes on.

Sample scenario 2: A sexy twist on the paid strip scenario is for it to be impromptu and free. For example, your girlfriend locks you in the garden, then gives you a decadent strip tease through the window where you can see her, but cannot touch her or get in the house until she says. Watch out for nosy neighbors!

Props: A sexy outfit is paramount—a g-string is the generally accepted norm. What you wear on top is up to you, but costumes can be worn such as a nurse's or maid's uniform. For shoes, stilettos or high heels are the best.

Role Plays for Beginners to Avoid

For starters, stay where you are both comfortable. There is a high degree of trust when role-playing involves things like light bondage. Always make sure to talk about what you plan to do prior to engaging in role play if there is a chance someone may feel less than happy and anything other than really turned on. It is important for both participants to be equally into it.

Rape role plays

Women often fantasize about being raped, but this doesn't actually mean they want to be raped in real life—they are very distinct and different things. It is more about the power and strength of being taken against her will, and for him, the power of control. A rape role play is something that could not possibly be done until you have built trust and know exactly what is required. It could end very badly, so don't rush into it. Safe words are needed so when one person is crying out "Stop! Stop!" you know when they actually mean it.

Bondage and discipline

This can be tons of fun, but care has to be taken to not embarrass, hurt, or offend your partner in real life by the treatment of them in a role play such as this. The rules have to be explicit and discussed prior to starting. Tying somebody up and teasing them with a feather is a bit different to putting a gimp mask on them and leading them around the house like a dog and forcing them to lick your boots and drink out of the toilet. Whipping and physical pain can also be pleasurable, but bear in mind there are special tools for spanking—drawing blood is not the point. Fetishes are normal and fun, but just be aware of what lengths you are asking somebody else to go to fulfill yours.

Play It Up

Role playing is a fantastic way to deepen and enrich your relationship. When both parties feel safe and secure, this playing often results in you both finding out more about each other—what you want done to you and done for you. Sexually, it broadens both of your horizons and allows your rich fantasy worlds to be unleashed (slowly!). If developed correctly—that is, comfortably and with sex appeal—role playing can become a successful way to get what you want out of your sex life without having to leave the house. Explore, laugh, and enjoy—you'll both be better for the experience.

RULE 11: MAKE YOUR MARK

Always leave a lasting impression. Armed with confidence, conversational skills, an aura of mystery, and a few choice moves, you're well on your way. Your ultimate goal: to be considered her greatest lover of all time. So take your time, hone your skills, pay attention to her, and adopt a few signature moves, and you'll be sure to never be forgotten.

BE HER GREATEST LOVER

If your woman has a group of gossiping friends, you'll want to make sure that you're on top of her A-list. Why should you be so concerned? Women kiss, and most usually tell—with great accuracy if you're a great lover, or great cruelty if you're not.

So how do you make your mark? You can be the best lover that she regrets losing; an ex-lover that she keeps coming back to because her current mate is nowhere close to the passionate lover you are; the lover that no woman would ever leave for another man—or the yearned-for lover inside her circle of friends.

That's right boys, if you play your cards right, you'll have women walking their dogs in front of your bachelor pad, hoping to see your lights on. Because once you earn the hallmark of a great lover, women will cherish your presence forever.

The only way to achieve this is by taking advantage of other men's natural laziness and do all the things a woman desires but has never experienced because her other lovers couldn't be bothered. And you can start by focusing on the body areas that other men neglect.

STIMULATE HER WITH 10 MOAN ZONES

As discussed earlier, one of the most frequent complaints that women have about male sexual behavior is that men are too genitally focused. Many men, particularly those in long-term relationships, think they should "get down and dirty" as soon as possible, so they can start enjoying the main course. Whether they're watching too much porn (which skips most foreplay), or listening to so-called "experts" who preach the primacy of clitoral or G-spot stimulation, men get the impression that, like themselves, women want to get genital stimulation as soon as their clothes come off.

However, this is not only wrong, but stimulating a woman's genitals before she becomes aroused through foreplay is usually a turn-off to most women!

This is because a woman's clitoris and genital area usually do not become conduits for sexual pleasure unless they are first activated by the increased blood flow that comes from arousal; that arousal usually begins with thorough, patient, and passionate attention to her other erogenous zones.

Thus, when men initiate sex, they need to supply that arousal before approaching their partner's genitals.

This is not as hard as it sounds. Most women are extremely sensitive to stimulation in certain often overlooked areas of their bodies; and a proper stimulation of these "moan zones" will produce exactly the kind of arousal that will then be manifested in vaginal lubrication and real readiness for a direct approach to her clitoris and genitals.

Here are the most important of these moan zones:

1. The Eyelid to Temple Zone

The area above and on her eyelid has a great concentration of nerve endings, and giving her light kisses along the arch of the lid and onto the temple is a great way to start foreplay. The spot between the outer corner of the eye and the cheekbone is also very sensitive. Thus, after some nice passionate kisses, a lover should let his lips wander all over her face, concentrating on these zones.

2. The Ear to Neck Zone

A woman's ears are among the most forgotten of pleasure zones, yet most women are extremely sensitive behind and over their earlobes. Using kisses and a licking tongue or gently stroking finger, trace the folds of her ears, nibble on her lobes, and gently stroke behind her ears and down the back of her neck.

3. The Neck to Shoulder Zone

Believe it or not, this is the primary moan zone! A majority of women get totally turned on by stimulation of the area from the back and sides of their neck to the ends of their shoulder blades. Some women can even orgasm from stimulation just in this area! Here, you can be a little less gentle: hard kisses, even love bites, and firm massage of this moan zone will be appreciated; the more time you spend here, the louder her moans will be. Try this with your lover: Approach her unawares from behind, then plant rows of kisses from the back of her neck down her shoulders.

4. The Navel to "V" Zone

Most women fantasize about being held in a firm manly grip, so don't be afraid to put your hands on or around her waist. Holding her from behind (while kissing the back of her neck), run your hands from her ribs to her pelvic bones, kneading and massaging the area in between. Let your hands roam all over the "V" zone, that triangular area from her hipbones to the top of her genitals (but hold off on grabbing those genitals just yet!).

5. The "Treasure Trail" Zone

The most sensitive area of a woman's lower torso is the aptly named Treasure Trail. This is the crease or line that extends across a woman's lower abdomen from one hipbone to the other, passing right over the top of the region covered with pubic hair (in its unshaved state). Make sure your kisses and fingers explore this "trail" before reaching her genitals.

6. The Foot Zone

This is a conditional moan zone. Some women are self-conscious about their feet and might be reluctant to allow you to pay court to them. For many others, however, it is a very erotic area. You can test your partner's attitude towards it and try to remove any reluctance by bathing her feet, then drying them on a soft towel. Move from there to a thorough massage of the feet using edible massage oil; then, follow it with oral stimulation. Start slowly, tracing the line of the massage strokes, and let your tongue travel between and around each toe before taking it in your mouth. If she responds with moans, you have identified another prime target for arousing your partner.

7. The Behind the Knee Zone

The skin behind the knees is thin and soft and very responsive to touch because the nerves are close to the surface. Most women find that kissing and licking the crease directly behind the knee is very pleasurable—some even get shivery chills of excitement from such stimulation. From her feet, work your way to this zone and then focus on it.

8. The Sacral Crease Zone

One of the more erotic zones in a woman's body is the crease between the curve of her buttocks and the top of her thighs, known as the sacral crease. Stroking or running a finger along that crease usually produces a strong erotic response. If your lover is on all fours or on her stomach and you are pleasuring her from behind, it is good to tease that area with a line of kisses or licks, bringing your lips closer and closer to her vaginal area with each pass.

9. The Buttocks Zone

The buttocks themselves are a strong erogenous zone, but they need to be approached slowly, after the other moan zones have been stimulated. Light stroking or a teasing little squeeze while you are stimulating Zones 1 through 8 are fine, but save the hard stuff, like firm squeezing or light spanking, until you have your partner well warmed up.

10. The Inner Thigh Zone

This is the penultimate moan zone, the last area to be stimulated before moving to her genitals. Don't overlook it though, as soft kisses and light fingertip stroking from her knees right up to (but not including) her vulva and clitoris will send her into that loud moaning state that proclaims her readiness for genital stimulation. The teasing nature of such touches will be the spark that lights her fire, as anticipation is the key to feminine arousal.

Utilize Her Entire Body

Want to be known as a smooth operator and not just a genitally focused animal in bed? Work the "moan zones" and you'll soon have her begging you for more!

DOGGY-STYLE SIGNATURE MOVES

You have to keep on evolving your repertoire if you want to keep it fresh with her (and have your legend grow amongst her friends). Work these moves into the routine and you'll both be pleasantly surprised.

Master Your Moves

Some girls might balk at jumping right into doggie style—it is a bit impersonal. But once you get her to consent, you can reach into your newly stocked bag of tricks and show her a real good time.

This is the best way to develop your own signature moves. Take the moves that worked (that is, the things that made her go crazy) and build on them. How will you know if they worked? Look for small hints like bleeding scratches on your back, broken furniture, or voice loss on her part from all the screaming.

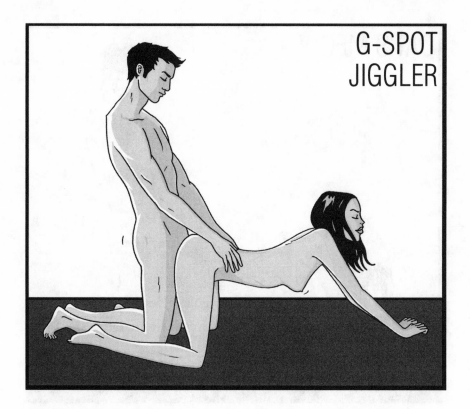

G-Spot Jiggler

One of the reasons women love getting it from behind is the depth of penetration and the ease at which you stimulate her G-spot. To get right at it, try the G-Spot Jiggler. Have her get on all fours on the bed. Enter her from behind and do nine short, hard pumps, and then one long, slow stroke. This will slide the head of your penis up against the top of her vagina (that's where her G-spot is, champ!). Mix up the number of short pumps, but be sure to always include that long, slow one. Odds are you won't have to remember; she'll be begging you for it.

CAT'S MEOW

Cat's Meow

If things are sizzling along, you can try this variation. Have her arch her back drastically, like a feline stretching. This position is called "The Cat's Meow" and it looks wickedly hot. It also sets up an angle that directs your shaft right at her G-spot. You won't be able to hammer away, but slow, rhythmic strokes will drive the girl crazy (which is the idea, after all).

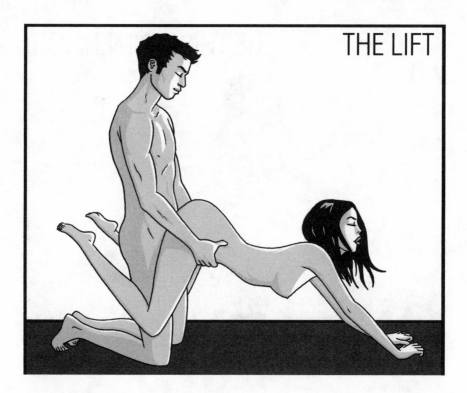

THE LIFT

The Lift

You can pick it up a notch by literally picking her up with a move aptly named "The Lift." Lock your arms under her legs and boost her up just a bit. This puts her in approximately the same angle as the "Cat's Meow," but allows you to bang a bit harder. Her G-spot will take a further pounding, but fear not; this is a very, very good thing for both of you.

Keep your hips still and use your arms to pull and push her toward you by her legs. Bodies will be slapping and she'll be in absolute ecstasy. You can also throw her a curveball by pulling out, hoisting her up even further and burying your face between her legs. Spend some quality time down there, then slide back into her for a bit, pull her up to your mouth, go back inside, and so on. She'll think about this routine for weeks.

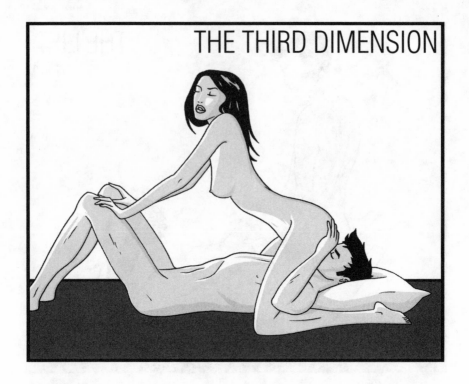

THE THIRD DIMENSION

The Third Dimension

Gauge how she is digging this and if all signs point to "yes," you can take it to the next level with "The Third Dimension." It is very similar to the routine described above, but you throw in a little backdoor action. Spend varying amounts of time giving her anal, vaginal, and oral stimulation. Or you can go for all three at the same time, using your mouth and both hands. All this attention and stimuli will make her feel like a goddess (or at least a porn star), and she will likely feel prompted to return the favor.

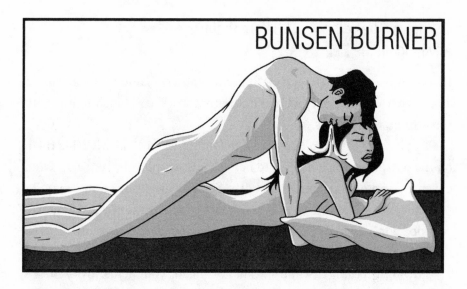

Bunsen Burner

The idea is to mimic the ascending flame of this laboratory staple by gradually easing into her.

Have her lie on her elbows with her butt in the air. Stand above her and slide just the tip in an inch or two, then tease it out a bit. Gradually work all the way in. Lean forward and combine it with some warm breathing techniques to heat things up to a boiling point. Brush her hair aside and bathe her neck in hot breath. Or lower your mouth near her ear and combine a bit of dirty talk with hot, husky breaths. Just don't ever let her hear the name of this move, at which point she will probably laugh you out of the bedroom.

8 THINGS WOMEN WISH MEN KNEW ABOUT SEX

Shaping yourself into a memorable lover hinges as much upon avoiding doing the wrong things as it involves doing the right things. Read on and learn how to avoid the little mistakes that all add up.

1. Always "Break the Seal" Before Putting Anything Inside Her.

If you and your girl are getting hot and bothered, and you want to do anything to her vagina, just make sure that when you touch it, it is with something wet. Always.

Apply your (or even her) saliva to two fingers and gently slide them on the outside of the entrance to her vagina, or spit into your hand and cover the end of your penis. Or both. Yes, she might be going crazy for you, but the wetness may not have reached the outside yet. Whatever you do, don't *ever* do it dry. Vaginas can be complex, multi-layered things!

Putting anything dry into a woman—fingers, your penis, toys—means she has to wriggle around to get her outside lips slippery. Even if this does only take 30 seconds, those 30 seconds of dry discomfort take her mind off how good everything else feels. It is a turn-on for her to feel "wet at first touch" and it can speed up the warm-up process.

2. Don't Bypass Her Neck or Ears.

The feeling she gets when you kiss, nuzzle, or lick her neck is likely 10 times as good as what you feel when she does the same to you. Her neck is one of the fastest ways to turn her on with the least effort. Be gentle with a moist tongue and soft lips, and you will have her moaning into *your* ear in no time. The front of her neck near her jugular is the most sensitive, but all over is good.

Ears are also a highly erogenous area, but there is a technique to giving good ear. *Some* heavy breathing, nibbling, and tongue action are all interesting and evocative sensations, whereas talking, loud "mwaack" kisses and slobbery licks are all definite no-nos. The trick to this is alternation; don't keep doing the same thing all the time. Instead, go from mouth to neck to ear to neck to breast, and so on.

3. Never Say Thank You for Fellatio or Sex.

This makes her feel like a hooker, so unless she is a hooker (or role playing!), refrain from thanking her. Show your appreciation in any other way you like, though, because she wants to know that she did a good job and you loved it. A thank you can come in many appropriate forms: "That was an excellent lick" or "You give the best head!" will suffice.

4. If You Orgasm Too Soon, It Is Very Disappointing for Her.

A woman *does* expect a man to be able to hold onto his orgasms long enough for her to get off. There is nothing more frustrating than premature ejaculation problems, and nothing has the potential to kill a relationship faster than lack of sexual satisfaction for either partner. If this is your problem, try to sort it out—go to a clinic, see a specialist, consult a sex therapist—whatever you do, don't let it go on too long. If you never got to have an orgasm, would you want to have sex?

Practice masturbating differently—get yourself nearly there, and then stop. Repeat. Practice until you get it right. If this doesn't help and you suspect it is a medical problem, seek help.

5. If You Don't Orgasm for Ages, It Can Be Annoying and Boring for Her.

Yes, yes, this is a sign that you're the *man*, right? A man who can keep going and going forever, taking his woman into the realms of ecstasy 10 times . . .

The truth is, 10 is pushing it. One is normally enough, two is good, three is a bonus. By then, she's spent, just like you after you ejaculate once.

Women don't dream of the man who can hold off orgasm all night long; they dream of the man who comes as she comes the first, second, or third time. She won't want to stop because obviously you're not done, but after all her fun is over and there isn't much hope of more, give it up already. If you are desensitized, give it a rest and come back for seconds later.

6. There Is More to a Breast Than Just a Nipple.

Most men think that the nipple is the best bit and aim straight for it. This is not necessarily true; the entire breast is an oft-neglected erogenous zone. While men are busy sucking, licking, stroking, and playing with the nipples (and unfortunately sometimes biting and twisting without prior permission), the rest is often forgotten.

There can be a sensuous buildup to hitting the nipple, like foreplay for the breast. Start on the outsides (avoiding armpits at all costs unless she likes armpit action) and work your way in with a tongue or finger. Circling brings the attention to the nipple, so when you do finally touch it, it is a great pleasure. Anticipation is the key, so use it to your advantage.

7. Trimmed Pubic Hair Is Better Even if She Says She Doesn't Care.

If you enjoy receiving oral sex, trim your pubic hair. Lots of women won't say anything, and if they say they don't care when asked, they are probably being truthful—only because they don't know what they're missing! Do it anyway. Trim it to about 5mm, and if you're really brave, try shaving your testicles.

This feels great for you and much better for her mouth; it is generally 20 times more enjoyable for everyone. Pubic hair is a real deterrent for a girl trying her best to lick your balls, and it can send her straight onto your penis if it gets too hairy down there. Surely you won't mind this, but there is no point in hastening the experience, now is there?

8. If You Approach Her in the Right Way, She Will Do Almost Anything.

A woman generally likes to feel in control, so when you suggest something out of the ordinary, she may react with suspicion. Who have you been talking to? Have you been sleeping with someone else to get these ideas? A defensive reaction to new ideas is a bad start. If you often encounter resistance, try a different tactic.

Magazine articles are a good way to educate her about options, especially if they are written by women. Find articles that have ordinary women talking about how good it was to have anal sex/have sex in a weird place/whatever you want to do, and get her to read it. Women's sex forums are also a good source. They give her time to read and absorb information without your opinion on the matter. Suggest it delicately, and then try to make her believe it was her idea in the first place.

No woman wants to be the one who won't play ball. Although there are things she may always say no to (anal sex and fisting perhaps), just remember it's a woman's prerogative to change her mind. Find the right method and you might just push her sexual experimentation button.

BUILD AND MAINTAIN A GOOD SEXUAL REPUTATION

Spreading the word of your bedroom prowess—or more to the point, having others spread it for you—is often an untapped source of action. The problem is that guys who brag about how good they are in bed usually aren't. Kudos to them for at least trying to boost their sexual rep; there are big rewards to be reaped if word gets out. But these guys are going about it all wrong. Be subtle, innovative, and resourceful, and you could find yourself saddled with a reputation as a top-shelf lover. And there are way worse things to be known as.

Project Sexual Confidence

Your confidence will speak for itself. That doesn't mean you should grind up against strange women at the bar, but the guy who clams up and blushes when the word "penis" crops up isn't going to come off very smooth.

You can project sexual savvy via certain cues. Women equate abilities on the dance floor with abilities in the sack, so learn some moves. Flailing about like a beached salmon will put the absolute kybosh on any chance of bedding the girl, so if you can't dance, suck it up and take some lessons. It's a fantastic investment, and you'll probably have a ton of fun taking them.

Ditto for food: You can convey sensuality in the way you approach eating; that is, with well-mannered relish and enthusiasm. Be adventurous and order food that involves slurping or the tactile experience of eating with your hands. She'll see how talented you are with your tongue and hands and she'll make the assumptions from there.

Finally, dress the part. The girl wearing the microskirt and lace shirt may be nice to look at, but she doesn't leave a lot to the imagination. The same goes for the dude in the wifebeater and skin-tight jeans. Wear something stylish and comfortable, but be sure that it "accidentally" floats up while you're dancing and gives her a quick sneak peek at what you've got.

Word of Mouth

The power of someone else's word cannot be overstated. Having another person brag about your prowess will do so much more to get you tail than the hottest dance moves ever could.

Ideally, you'll have a female friend creating the buzz about your sexual skills rather than a male friend. It'll be far more effective, as women know that we band together in these kinds of ventures. Your buddy—his best intentions aside—could end up squandering your chances.

In either case, the word of mouth needs to be delivered discreetly, and your presence as the motivation behind it needs to be invisible. Play it subtle; don't have your friend blurt out how well endowed you are, but have her casually mention to her friends how your ex won't stop badgering you to maintain a physical relationship.

The best route here is the natural one: Build your sexual reputation sincerely, and they will come. Make it memorable enough for her, and she'll pass on her experience to a few of her friends. And they tell five friends, who tell five friends, and so on . . . Soon enough, a fantastic web of ladies will know just how good you are at what you do. From there, it's up to you to reap what you sow. Happy reaping!